A 50 DAY

BREAKDOWNS
— AND —
BREAKTHROUGHS

JOE WOODYARD

© 2024 Joe Woodyard
BREAKDOWNS AND BREAKTHROUGHS

All rights reserved. No part of this publication may be reproduced, stored in a retrieval system, or transmitted in any form or by any means, electronic, mechanical, photocopying, recording, or otherwise without the prior permission of the publisher or in accordance with the provisions of the Copyright, Designs and Patents Act 1988 or under the terms of any license permitting limited copying issued by the Copyright Licensing Agency.

Scripture quotations taken from the Amplified® Bible (AMPC), Copyright © 1954, 1958, 1962, 1964, 1965, 1987 by The Lockman Foundation. Used by permission.

Scripture quotations taken from the New King James Version (NKJV)®. Copyright © 1982 by Thomas Nelson. Used by permission. All rights reserved.

Scripture quotations taken from THE MESSAGE (MSG), copyright © 1993, 2002, 2018 by Eugene H. Peterson. Used by permission of NavPress. All rights reserved. Represented by Tyndale House Publishers, a Division of Tyndale House Ministries.

Scripture quotations taken from the Holy Bible, New Living Translation (NLT), copyright ©1996, 2004, 2015 by Tyndale House Foundation. Used by permission of Tyndale House Publishers, Inc., Carol Stream, Illinois 60188. All rights reserved.

Scripture quotations taken from the Holy Bible, New International Version®, (NIV®). Copyright ©1973, 1978, 1984, 2011 by Biblica, Inc.TM Used by permission of Zondervan. All rights reserved worldwide.

Scripture quotations taken from The ESV® Bible (The Holy Bible, English Standard Version®), © 2001 by Crossway, a publishing ministry of Good News Publishers. Used by permission. All rights reserved.

Library of Congress Control Number: 2024900708

ISBN: 979-8-218-33994-4

Published by:
Resurgence Publishing, LLC
P.O. Box 514
Goshen, OH 45122
www.resurgencebooks.org

Cover Design: Aaftab Sheikh

Printed in the United States of America

DEDICATION

This book is dedicated to my Dad., who went from the farm fields of Athens, Ohio to the battlefields of Vietnam. From that beginning, you ultimately became the hero to a family, a church, and—in our eyes—the ages to come.

May the angels in heaven report to you each day a life is changed upon reading Day 43. I asked you, while you were undergoing chemotherapy, to write a devotional to be placed in this book. You not only wrote it, but did so well that it is unquestionably my favorite part of this endeavor. Mom and I have already dogeared your devotional page. You didn't know it at the time, but your words, "all is not lost," have been an anchor to the family. We know where you are, you are not lost. See you on graduation day.

—Joe

Contents

Three Words to Change Your Life 12

Lessons From David 30
   DAY 1—Beware of Idle Time 30
   DAY 2—The Danger of a Compliment 32
   DAY 3—A Campaign of Kindness 34
   DAY 4—The Lord is my Shepherd 36
   DAY 5—Giants Still Fall 38
   DAY 6—David and the Giant 40

Lessons From Peter 42
   DAY 7—Behold 42
   DAY 8—"That Your Faith May Not Fail" 44
   DAY 9—When You Turn Back 46
   DAY 10—The Time of Testing 48

Lessons From Joseph 52
   DAY 11—Joseph and the All-Season Coat 52
   DAY 12—Not Everyone Will Like You! 54
   DAY 13—Joseph Had a Dream 56
   DAY 14—A Night in a Pit 58

Lessons From Nehemiah 60
   DAY 15—You Have to Start Somewhere 60
   DAY 16—Loose Lips Sink Ships 62
   DAY 17—Troublesome Times 64
   DAY 18—A Mind to Work 66
   DAY 19—The Power to Ignore 68
   DAY 20—Wanted: a Life with a Purpose 70

Lessons From Daniel 74
   DAY 21—Convictions 74
   DAY 22—I Dare You 76
   DAY 23—Do It Anyway 78
   DAY 24—Image is Not Everything 80
   DAY 25—Do Not Be Afraid 82

Lessons From Paul **84**
  DAY 26—Discovering Your Purpose Through Burnout . 84
  DAY 27—Your Wounds Are Useful 86
  DAY 28—Be Strong In the Lord 88
  DAY 29—Dress for Success 90
  DAY 30—Hard Places 92
  DAY 31—Sing Anyway 94
  DAY 32—Stay Stirred 96
  DAY 33—The Valedictorian 98
  DAY 34—Joshua 100

Lessons From Mary **102**
  DAY 35—A Season to Believe 102

Breakthrough with the Attributes of God **104**
  DAY 36—The Affirmation of God 104
  DAY 37—In Awe of God 108
  DAY 38—The Fatherhood of God 110
  DAY 39—The Faithfulness of God 112
  DAY 40—The Authority of God 114

Passion Week **116**
  DAY 41—God's Passover, Beginning at Sundown 116
  DAY 42—Jesus Went First 120
  DAY 43—All is Not Lost 122
  DAY 44—Roman Soldiers 124
  DAY 45—Simon of Cyrene 126
  DAY 46—The Centurion 128

The Temptation Of Jesus **130**
  DAY 47—Stones into Bread 130
  DAY 48—You Don't Look Like a Child of God 132
  DAY 49—The Danger of the High Places 136
  DAY 50—Our Final Breakthrough 138

About the Author **140**

Recommendations

"My close friend and fellow minister, Joe Woodyard, has, with the heart of a true pastor, given us a devotional book that is solidly grounded in the Scriptures and filled with encouragement for anyone seeking the personal presence and peace of God. Pastor Joe's extensive knowledge of God's Word and its proper application to hungry hearts today, together with his highly engaging writing style, will richly bless, strengthen, and comfort all who take the time to quarry the valuable treasures contained in these timely devotionals."

—*Bobby G. Duncan*
Brunswick, Ohio

"I believe you will find this 50 day devotional a wealth of inspiration. Each days' brief breakthrough is rich in content, scripture, and illustration.

I like the authors observation in the introduction that says "sometimes it's not until we have something to compare with that we know how good one is above the other." This devotional does that exactly - weaving stories from scripture with life lessons in a very productive, helpful, and inspiring way.

The reader will be blessed each morning with these devotions offering breakthroughs in these challenging days we live in. Be encouraged!"

—*Dr Bruce Philippi, Lead Pastor*
Journey Life Center
Mansfield, Ohio

"I am excited to recommend Joe Woodyard's book, "Breakdowns and Breakthroughs: A 50 Day Devotional." In this inspiring devotional, Joe takes readers on a journey of spiritual renewal and empowerment. Drawing from his own experiences and insights as a pastor, Joe skillfully navigates the complexities of life's challenges, offering powerful prayers and transformational truths to guide readers from breakdowns to breakthroughs.

What sets this book apart is its authenticity and relatability. Woodyard shares candidly about his own struggles and triumphs, making each devotional entry feel like a personal conversation with a trusted friend. Whether you're facing loss, adversity, or uncertainty, "Breakdowns and Breakthroughs" provides the encouragement and wisdom needed to overcome obstacles and embrace God's promises for a brighter future.

I highly recommend this book to anyone seeking hope, healing, and spiritual growth. It's a must-read for anyone ready to embark on a journey of transformation and discover the breakthroughs waiting on the other side of breakdowns."

—Jeff Wolf
Speaker and Best-Selling Author
Cincinnati, Ohio

LETTER TO THE READER

It was during my spring semester at community college that my love for books reached its peak. The class was "Intro to Short Fiction," and our teacher, Mr. Halstead, was in his late 50s. He epitomized the typical English professor, philosophical to the core. We would arrange our chairs in a circle and discuss our subjective takeaways from the assigned short stories. I was captivated by Melville, Hemingway, and F. Scott Fitzgerald, who, for a time in my life, stood unrivaled. Books became the medium through which God reached me. In that environment, I began to perceive the Bible differently. The best of human literature seemed to lack something. Even the famed authors couldn't match the beauty of scripture. Here, I had been exposed to the best author all my life (the Bible) and hadn't realized it.

Sometimes, it's not until we have a point of comparison that we understand the superiority of one over the other. To me, their prose was an escapism from reality. In reading the scriptures, I found an escape from sin. Why is this important for the reader? Partly because it was my love of the short story that marked my turning point. Just a paragraph or a well-written sentence can resonate with you indefinitely. These are short writings. This is not an academic work or doctrinal dissertation. I have eschewed flowery speech because that wouldn't be true to myself. These devotionals are my fish and loaves, which I have placed in the hands of the Lord—with the hopes that he will multiply them.

Joe Woodyard

Preface

In 2017, I began experiencing some aches and pains and did what I suggest you never do—Google it! Naturally, after my "Google research," I was convinced that I had a terminal disease. Simultaneously, alongside the physical discomfort, I was dealing with a strange spiritual battle involving issues like offense and pride. Unknowingly, I had opened the door to an attack. The medical world refers to such phenomena as psychosomatic, meaning your brain can produce feelings of sickness that aren't actually present. The mind is indeed powerful. My aches plunged me into extreme paranoia. I visited the doctor two days in a row, seeking assurance that everything was okay. He prescribed anxiety medication. I took it for one day, and it caused my entire body to shake. For a while, I was physically exhausted from fear.

Once my wife discovered my fears (and you have to understand her nature), she took authoritative action—rebuking the devil. During my struggle, we would take communion. She played sermons for me to listen to and gradually nursed me back to spiritual health. The recovery wasn't immediate; about 3-4 months of fear persisted. I continued my ministry work, but it was the most challenging period of my life. Here's where it gets unusual: the night of communion, after praying together, my wife claimed she saw a dark figure emerge from our master bathroom, exit, pause, glance our way, and laugh. She immediately interpreted the incident. (My wife is not given to sensationalism. She is very logical and practical, so I believed her when she said she saw something.) She told me, "You're letting the devil have fun with you. He is attacking your mind." That's when I realized that I had attracted a tormentor as I grappled with pride and offenses. That figure never returned. I'm better now. I hope I haven't scared you off and that you're still reading this. Here's what I learned: That attack made me wiser. I've become more sympathetic, appreciate people more than ever, and cultivated kindness, patience, and courage in my ministry. I believe my ministry reached a new level after that experience. Lastly, I realized that my greatest breakthrough came after my greatest breakdown. I believe the same will be true for you!

Introduction

Are you headed for a breakdown?

Anthony Gatto began juggling at the age of 3 and started performing at age 10. Once a childhood prodigy, he now holds nine world records. By many, Anthony is considered the greatest juggler in the world. In an interview, he admitted that for him, juggling provides a sense of value: "Down deep inside, everyone wants to be recognized." I don't know much about juggling, but I can relate to the search for value. Like Anthony Gatto, do we juggle a hectic life for notoriety? Is your schedule overloaded to make more money, gain more recognition, fame, or acceptance? What are you juggling back and forth? School, work, your big dreams? I admit, I am no juggler, but I am a good multitasker. I am adept at carrying books, my car keys, and a hot cup of coffee all in the same hand a recipe for disaster, I know. We wouldn't overload life's capacities as much if we could just slow down.

Slowing down is important for your safety. When we don't, we become susceptible to an emotional breakdown. I remember as a child, before heading into kindergarten, my mom sent me off to safety town. It was a basic instructional course on "how not to get hurt," among other things. It was common-sense training, teaching you to slow down. At any age, we should stop and survey the risks and rewards before making any major decisions. A devotional is just that slowing down and preparing each day with a thought from scripture. The Bible is the safety town for our everyday lives. As you read, there is no guarantee that you won't bump your ego or scrape your spiritual knees.

I chose fifty as the number of devotionals for the simple reason that in the Old Testament, fifty is the number of freedom, freedom from fear and all that holds you back. In the New Testament, it was on the fiftieth day that the Holy Spirit showed up and created a group of people the likes of which the world had never seen! So, meditate, see if you relate, and hopefully learn as you read over the next fifty days. I believe you will experience breakthroughs.

Before you get started, I want you to be reminded of three words that will help you love people to health. These are common words in Christianity. We sometimes use them loosely, but it's in practicing them that breakthroughs happen around you. I know what you're thinking: "I bought this book, and I want to read 'How to Receive a Breakthrough.' Where are the sword-wielding saints? Where are the lion's dens and sea walkers?" They are here, just not yet. These three words will help you build a system of success. If you want to be like Jesus and see what brought breakthroughs in the lives of the men and women of the Bible, keep reading. In each character devotion, these virtues were common; they were undeniable gifts of the Holy Spirit. The help they received from the Holy Spirit was the difference-maker. The three words? Kindness, patience, and courage.

Three Words to Change Your Life

Three words have the power to change your life. Jesus concluded his life on the Cross with just three words: "It is finished." In essence, this means "paid in full." Jesus intended for you to hear those words. What if I told you that Jesus has already paid for your mistakes and sins in advance? Wouldn't that make you feel better about yourself and your future? Wouldn't you feel somewhat relieved, knowing that your debts have been paid for? Jesus paid for your sins, and He also paid for your victories. That vacation of peace you're seeking? Paid in full. That jar of joy? Paid in full. What about a ride down the road of contentment or a walk down the path of abundant supply? They are already paid for in full. Jesus paid it all. These three words are crucial to your breakthrough.

How do you access these gifts? First, you need to accept the life-giver. Jesus is the life-giver. As stated in John 10:10 NIV, "The thief comes only to steal and kill and destroy; I have come that they may have life, and have it to the full."

My three words are not as impactful as "it is finished," but they may be helpful to you at some point in your journey. Living them out won't directly redeem anyone. Still, perhaps they will aid someone in finding Jesus along the way.

Be Kind

"Be kind and encouraging because everyone you meet is in a battle." Warren Wiersbe

On a hill overlooking the northwest shore of the Sea of Galilee, a Jewish carpenter turned rabbi settled on a flat place to deliver what would become known as the greatest sermon ever preached: the Sermon on the Mount. The crowds quieted. Had they really heard Jesus say, "Turn the other cheek if someone strikes you"? Keep on forgiving? Pray for those who spite you? These were revolutionary thoughts. The offer was kindness. The promise was help, but He must first have your heart for it to make sense. Kindness would become one of the mainstays in the Messiah's ministry. Is it yours?

Jesus taught the disciples to be gentle. When the brothers James and John sought thunder, Jesus insisted on mercy. Kindness is often displayed through our encouragement towards one another. Being kind means allowing someone's troubles to find shelter under your generosity. Jesus exemplified this every day with a gentle touch in His ministry. Matthew tells us that early in the ministry of Jesus, He had a mender's touch. "A bruised reed He will not break, and a smoking flax He will not quench." (Matthew 12:20 KJV).

Every day, we encounter those on the cusp of giving up. Jesus' intention was never to "finish them off." No one was too far gone. Prodigals, prostitutes, or hot-tempered fishermen, it didn't matter; Jesus had an answer for them all. His mission was to heal the broken-hearted, bring sight to the blind, and set the captives free. In the world Jesus lived in, there were many hurting people. Isaiah 53 speaks candidly about how Jesus was acquainted with sorrow and grief throughout His ministry. Broken people surrounded Him, and they will show up before you too.

Many years ago, I heard the following story: In the early 1970s, a Vietnam veteran called home with nervous anticipation. "Hi, Mom, I'm coming home!" "That's great, honey, we are so excited to see you." "Mom, I met a friend here. He doesn't have anywhere else to go. Can I bring him home to live with us for a while?" "Well, sure, honey. But Mom, there's something I need to tell you. There was a terrible explosion. My friend lost his legs. He's in a wheelchair." The phone call went silent. "Well, honey, I don't think that would be a good idea; that would be a lot of work, and we have so much to take care of already." Shortly after, the phone call ended. There was no friend; the call was from the son, who was the one who had lost his legs in the war. The story becomes even sadder because of the rejection; the young war hero committed suicide. Be kind. We never know who is hurting and from what. Let someone find refuge under your generosity.

I have been in ministry for nearly thirty years. It's not very often that someone tells me, 'That message you preached 10 years ago was unforgettable, Pastor...'. But what many people do remember are the words shared in their time of need. They recall the funeral sermon with an illustration that helped them cope with grief, or the time I visited them in the hospital.

When my father was battling a particular sickness, I had a couple of people from our church come to me in tears. "I am praying for your dad; I remember when your dad came to my family's funeral." You might think that's what pastors should do. They should, but the true gem in this story is how a family found Christ from a surprise pastoral visit.

People remember what you do for them more than what you say. It's often said, 'people don't care how much you know until they know how much you care.' That's why I believe a believer's feet and hands should be more active than their voice. Kindness leaves a lasting mark, just as a scar reminds you of a past accident or injury. Kindness leaves an imprint on people's hearts, a reminder of where love once visited. Be kind.

Kindness assumes others need grace. It is expressed through sensitivity. We should intentionally practice being considerate. Why? Because everyone is facing a battle of some sort. Kindness displayed is essentially saying, "I too have walked in your shoes," "I understand life's difficulties." In being kind, we are sensitive to what we don't know about a person.

This is another reason the Bible instructs us, "Let no corrupt communication proceed out of your mouth, but that which is good to the use of edifying, that it may minister grace unto the hearers." (Ephesians 4:29 KJV). Edifying means to build up, to encourage one another with grace. We don't know what burdens others are carrying. Are they dealing with financial struggles? Perhaps mental or physical spousal abuse? Is there a child battling substance abuse? A sickness in the home?

Many years ago, I heard a story that has stayed with me. It was in a large congregation. "The commotion was hard to tolerate. Of all places to be noisy, in the middle of a Sunday morning church service was not the place," she thought. Sitting in her pew, she struggled to bite her tongue, periodically looking back, wondering how a father could let his children be so disruptive. The dad paid no attention to the kids wandering around the aisle behind her. He just stared, as if lost in another world.

The service ended, and she couldn't resist approaching the man. "Sir, in church, you should try to control your kids a little more." He was still sitting in the pew and replied after a pause, "Oh, I apologize. I guess I never noticed. I'm just not with it today. My apologies, my mind is elsewhere; I'm just trying to figure out how to tell my three children that their mom passed away last night. I just thought I would come to church looking for some direction." Can you imagine how remorseful she must have felt?

Kindness recognizes that everyone is battling something. It is always looking for someone to lift up. The book of Hebrews encourages us to support others, for we must never tear down what God is trying to restore. "Lift up the feeble hands and the knees that hang down, and make straight paths for your feet." (Hebrews 12:12-13 KJV).

HEAVY LIFTERS NEEDED

In the Bible, God designed an organized pattern of worship. For the Old Testament saints, a tabernacle and tent were created for worship. Overseeing the magnificent design and mobility of the traveling worship center were three groups of priests. But only one group, the Levites, were assigned the lifting and carrying duties of the main structure of the Tabernacle. They were responsible for tearing down and assembling the worship tent from city to city and every stopping point in between.

We may have never realized this, but heavy lifting was required in preparing the worship service in the Old Testament. Even the preparation required a priestly touch. Every church has heavy lifters. You know who you are. You are the person who gets the call to open the church for the funeral home, set up the stage for VBS week, check the roof for missing shingles, or take the evangelist to the airport. These are essential people for making the service a success. They are the heavy lifters. They have been assigned to make the worship service everything God intended it to be.

Rightfully so, without the heavy lifters in our past and present, we wouldn't be enjoying the blessings we do now. 'A WOUNDED SPIRIT WHO CAN BEAR?' The heaviest lifting of all is encouraging discouraged people. Those left in the wake of difficult circumstances, tragedies, and hardships. Lifting up discouraged people doesn't get much heavier than that. Thank God for today's heavy lifters.

Heavy lifters today are encouragers within the body of Christ. Most often, they are men and women who have come through some great trials themselves. Job's wife told him to throw in the towel. It was Goliath who shouted at David, 'You have no chance.' Early one morning, Peter told Jesus, 'We have fished all night and caught nothing.' But these are the moments that make the story more like your story. Life hands you a reason to quit. When excuses are easier than starting again, you have two directions to go at that point: quit or keep going. Encouragers shout, 'Keep going, you're almost there.'

Job got it all back. The giant fell. And Peter caught so many fish that he shared with others. That's the part you need to focus on. Chances are very good that you will have a breakthrough.

THE BARNABAS TOUCH

Barnabas in the New Testament is called the 'son of consolation,' meaning the son of encouragement. He had a reputation for bolstering the ministry. He possessed a gift for connecting and promoting the early church ministries. We could certainly use a few more Barnabases today. What was the Barnabas dynamic? The ability to listen. Barnabas believed in Paul. He paid little attention to yesterday's mistakes and recognized today's potential. There is no doubt Barnabas would be criticized today by some for using 'anybody in ministry.' Barnabas had the heart to look at the gifting inside a person and open the door of opportunity for them. He handed Paul a church community that needed his ministry, his wit, and wisdom. Paul was asked to accompany Barnabas to the church of Antioch, with no mention of Paul's past, only his present. That is the 'Barnabas touch' always striving to connect ministry to mission fields. Barnabas must have been humble and selfless. Many ministers would fear adding a dynamic ministry like Paul's, worried that they may be under-appreciated. Barnabas, however, had been touched with an inner security. To be secure in oneself is to be at peace with your abilities and limitations. He was a secure man. Anyone who dreams for another must first be secure in themselves. Thus, Barnabas was gifted in connecting the right ministry to the right church.

While pastoring for over fifty years, my dad would often invite our denominational state officials to visit the church. Most were unforgettable; Gale Barnett was no exception. He was tall and slender with a Texas accent and soft-spoken mannerisms. He was sincere, gentle, and kind. I was only 12 or 13 years old when I accompanied Dad and Gale to a local historic restaurant. They went there to talk about church matters. My attention span was short, and I don't recall much of the conversation. What I do remember is that after Gale left, everyone was happier. Both of my parents shared how he encouraged them. Gale didn't talk as much as he listened. That is what I took away that day. Encouragers are not necessarily known for their inspirational speeches, but for their ability to listen. That's part of the Barnabas dynamic. Bryant McGill wisely wrote, 'One of the most sincere forms of respect is actually listening to what another has to say.'

"Be kind and compassionate to one another, forgiving each other, just as in Christ God forgave you." (Ephesians 4:32 NIV). Kindness is having your shoelaces tied when you can't. (I'll explain). Kristi Huffman was my first real friend. She had two older brothers, and it was evident they played a role in raising her. She was tough, both physically and emotionally. She lived across the street from my aunt, where I spent many afternoons during my summers. Once school started, Kristi and I shared the same recess time. I won't waste time saying I struggled in elementary school. More than just struggled, I hated it. As I got older, I realized it wasn't school I disliked, but leaving home and my parents. Those recess breaks were my favorite part of the day, a chance to release my emotions. I would walk around, fighting back tears, as the days seemed so long. Then there was Kristi Huffman. I don't think she ever cried. She was free-spirited and as tough as nails. Kristi would walk around and listen to me every day, asking, 'How much longer until school is out.' But what will always be etched in my mind is the times I needed my shoes tied, and Kristi did it. Not being able to tie your shoes in the first grade was a recipe for panic. She would kindly bend on one knee and tie my shoe, and my panic would subside. To this day, I tie my shoes like a left-hander, even though I am right-handed. I learned from watching her, despite it being unorthodox. Was the kindness in just tying my shoes? No, what was even kinder was that she never laughed. Kristi never made a public announcement to all the classmates, 'Everyone get over here; Joe can't tie his own shoes.' Looking back, kindness is seen in your willingness to hide someone's flaws. Kindness is carrying and covering someone's burdens, even if just until they can tie their own shoes. Kindness is essentially the intuition you have to care for others, hiding their weaknesses behind your strengths. You will not only win battles when you exude a spirit of kindness; you will win friends. D. T. Niles had it right when he said, 'Christianity is just one beggar telling another beggar where he found bread.'

BE PATIENT

"Patience applied to our lives is like allocating little pieces of trust each day until your dream takes place."

Most basketball players, especially point guards, dread it—it's relentless, always attacking, making you sweat more than a business deal deadline. It's none other than the full-court press! Former Indiana Hoosiers basketball coach Bob Knight was known for his unpredictable temperament, but one consistent aspect of his coaching was his late-game full-court pressure. His theory? Tired and out-of-shape players make mistakes late in the game. The objective of the full-court press was to change the tempo of the game. The faster the pace, the more room for turnovers. The key to beating the press is having a point guard who knows when to dribble and when to pass. The point guard is responsible for maintaining the pace, keeping the team in rhythm, and keeping the team calm. Great point guards have the ability to maintain the tempo and overcome the pressure by the opponent. Stubbornly, they play at their pace, not the opponents'. Similarly, one of the great challenges for believers is to live in the rhythms of grace.

The enemy and our flesh would love nothing more than to disrupt our pace, to pressure us into turning over our peace and joy. Jesus taught the seriousness of living life outside the boundaries of patience and endurance. In warning the disciples, he explained that the end days would be a time where many people are overrun by fear. Surfeiting and reckless lifestyles would be the undoing of many, with fatigue and mistakes replacing discretion and healthy choices. Full-court pressure applied nonstop to our spiritual life is like living every hour under the pressure to get somewhere God never intended you to be. So, slow down, stop wrestling, and be patient.

Many years ago, while speaking to a packed-out stadium, Reverend Billy Graham shared this story: "A young man went to visit his friend in California. Both were accomplished Olympic high divers. Unable to sleep one night, he decided to practice some late-night diving with the moon to his back. Climbing the ladder, he noticed every time he stretched out his hands over the swimming pool, he saw the shadow of a cross. Two or three times he stretched out at the edge of the diving board, each time seeing the appearance of a shadowy cross several feet below. Curious, he decided to climb down and take a closer look before diving. Once at the bottom of the ladder and closer to the pool, to his amazement, he discovered the pool was empty. He was so moved by this realization that the Olympic diver soon gave his heart to Christ. His lifelong testimony when anyone asked what changed him was a humble remark that the reflection of the cross saved his life."

God does not always move us forward. Sometimes His plan is to slow us down, knowing the dangers that may lie ahead.

Waiting On A Promise

When it comes to a promise in your life, you are either waiting for it or wrestling over it. Very rarely do we do both. As a pastor, I have concluded that many believers are either in the state of working for the Lord or worrying about where to start. Most churches have two categories of members: one group struggling just to stay in the pew, while the others are eager to serve. More than at any other time, a pastor must exercise patience while one group heals and the other helps. This involves carefully nursing those who need growth and strength and assertively limiting the "serving group" from burnout. Patience is possibly the greatest healing practice for the soul and mind, administered by Jesus through the Holy Spirit. Jesus said, "In your patience, possess your souls." (Luke 21:18, KJV).

What was Jesus saying? Your emotions will directly wage war with you more often than a spiritual opponent. It is likely that the "enemy of our souls" will try to agitate your emotional stability, using deadlines, peer pressure, and trouble next door, all in an attempt to hurry us into exhaustion. The dark forces against us have a favorite race, the "rat race," pushing you to the limits. When Satan can't orchestrate your undoing by sinning, he tries to by exhaustion. Patience is the power of self-control. The biggest battles we face stem from the lack of self-control. Don't allow the external to control you. Allow the Holy Spirit to dwell richly in you, bringing the costly and extravagant help that Christ promised. Patience is the investment made in maintaining a sound mind. Jesus wants you to be patient.

Time is God's way of organizing your life. The world is a big place with lots of people, and many people equal diversity and differences. Somehow, God makes all these diversities work together like a magneto on an engine, creating a spark and "voilà," there you have it, perfect timing. "When the timing is right, I the Lord God will make it happen.." (Isaiah 60:22). Timing is essential to your very existence. The earth rotates on its axis in a time sequence. Your heart beats in rhythm or time. In your personal life, think of it this way: if you had not gone to class that day or to that birthday party, you would have never met him or her. What about the flat tire that made you late? Perhaps that's why you averted that tragic car accident. The person of your dreams most often walked down the hall of destiny at the same time as you. Coincidence? I am told that in Biblical Hebrew, there is no such word as coincidence. This is not to say that we don't choose and have no free autonomy in our decisions. Rather, we must see our life through the lens of God's providence. As free people, we decide with full accountability for our actions. Yet, be aware that the opportunities that arise or the doors that slam shut help us explain the omniscience of God. God not only controls the affairs of our day-to-day lives but also manages the traffic we get ourselves into. He is transcendent, outside of time, not relying on anything for His existence, but He chooses to step into your life at just the right time. The story of the Good Samaritan helps us recognize God's timing.

Laws Of The Good Samaritan: He Came At The Right Time

"And by chance there came down a certain priest that way: and when he saw him, he passed by on the other side. And likewise a Levite, when he was at the place, came and looked on him, and passed by on the other side. But a certain Samaritan, as he journeyed, came where he was: and when he saw him, he had compassion on him," (Luke 10:31-33 KJV).

You must realize that your journey is not by chance or completely fatalistic. "As he journeyed.." (Luke 10:33). This suggests a purposeful path in life.

Pay attention. Keep an eye out for those wounded and hurting. Often, this is where your Christianity is meant to be expressed. "..And when he saw him.." (Luke 10:33). Being observant and responsive is key.

Remember, someone you help may have been passed up by someone else who could have assisted. "..He passed by on the other side.." (Luke 10:31). Your actions can make a significant difference.

Compassion is the realization that the situation could have been yours. "...And he came where he was.. and had compassion.." (Luke 10:33). Identifying with others in their suffering is a foundational aspect of compassion. Jesus, our Good Samaritan, exemplified this, telling us to "Go and do likewise."

Of all the truths this parable holds, don't overlook the fact that if the Good Samaritan had been a little earlier, he could have been the one robbed. What we learn from the parable of the "good Samaritan" is that timing is critical for both your safety and opportunity. Trust the process; God is guiding you to where you belong.

God Works In You

The passion you have for your profession or life's calling, where did it come from? Someone influenced you. Nearly every school teacher asks their elementary students, "What do you want to be when you grow up?" How do they know? Something or someone has influenced their decision. Some answer unrealistically, while others will have no clue until sometime in their adult life. But don't miss the fact that God is actively giving us inspiration and hints to find what we love. What brings us fulfillment? Why we choose what to do is a complicated answer, yet still at the heart, we must admit, "it is God who works in you both to will and to do for His good pleasure." (Philippians 2:13, NKJV).

All throughout scripture, God is participating in history. Today, as then, God is methodically pursuing you to align you with a purpose within His redemptive order. For example, one of the many ways God directs our affairs is by dream and by vision. It doesn't take long to read in the Bible where God is sending dreams to men like Daniel and Joseph. Pilate's wife dreamed prior to her husband making the biggest mistake in his life. How about you? Are you aware that millions of people dream each night? Dreams are one way in which God helps direct us. Dreams are clearly a gift from God. They warn us of danger and hopefully precipitate prayer. Dreams from God help us influence our decisions when we are unclear on what steps to take. Make no mistake about it,

God is actively working in your life. Dreams in the Bible were often given months or years in advance of their fulfillment, causing men like Joseph to wait patiently until the fullness of time arrived. Your promises aren't hopeless; they may just be tarrying in the timeline of God's handiwork.

Abraham and Sara had to wait until they were 90 to birth Isaac. Joseph waited on time and, harder yet, he had to wait through many trials. He was patient through jealousy, prison, and a seven-year famine. Moses waited 80 years to captain Israel. David was patient among the promises of God; he also sat patiently at several stops along the way. Patience doesn't imply inactivity, just the opposite. Patience happens when we have to be busy with our second or third passion. When the number one place we want to be isn't ready yet. When we wait on God, we are likely mending our nets for the greater catch. Think about David never staying in the same home for long. He patiently waited for advancement while in a shepherd's field, a cave, an enemy's doorstep before finally becoming king in Jerusalem. Keep waiting. David wrote, "Wait on the Lord. Be of good courage and he will strengthen your heart." (Psalms 27:14).

God told Moses to take off his shoes. "Stay awhile," the Lord wanted some time with Moses. The Lord used a burning bush to gain his attention. Moses did a lot of waiting; his life was broken up into three periods of 40 years. Basically, he received a thorough education on waiting. Forty years in Egypt, forty years in training under Jethro, his father-in-law, and forty years in the wilderness. Among the many lessons he learned in his 120-year history of following God, he learned that God has victories planned, and we must wait on His timing. Patience is the antidote to pressure. Leaders are measured by their ability to handle pressure. Moses was being prepared to carry the burden of an infant nation. Strong leaders in the Bible were often assigned a layover.

JOB, THE MAN WHO WAITED

Job's great power, you ask? Job was willing to wait! Job was brilliantly patient. The fascinating book of Job has inspired millions to trust God through their trials. It offers the best understanding we have in the Old Testament on suffering. Interestingly, Job is the example James chose to use in describing patience.

"Behold, we count them happy which endure. Ye have heard of the patience of Job, and have seen the end of the Lord; that the Lord is very pitiful, and of tender mercy." (James 5:11, KJV).

That's quite a compliment. Job, who lost everything, is described as patient. He did a lot of waiting; waiting for an answer to why all this suffering had befallen him, waiting for his "Redeemer" to stand up for him in the last days, as he confidently proclaimed, "for I know that my Redeemer lives." Job waited for his wife to understand that God did not set out to destroy him. He waited for his sores to heal, for his heart to mend a little more each hour. Job waited for his friends to show up, then waited for them to leave. Finally, when the wait was over, God visited him in a strong voice. "Where were you at the beginning, Job? What do you know about running the world?"

The truth easily overlooked in Job is that the running of the world is very complex. God organizes the messes humanity leaves behind. Daily, hourly, every passing click of the clock, God arranges your story. In Job, we are reminded of a God who can reserve the weather for judgment, pouring out the rains at just the right time, controlling the kingdoms of this world with His command. Who is like our God, who gives animals their instincts and makes the heavens display His handiwork? Most impressively, how can a Holy God rule a world where so much evil takes place and yet allow us to retain our free will? In the New Testament, Paul in the book of Romans answers this question philosophically, ".. for we know that He makes everything work together..". In another place, the writer of Ecclesiastes says, "He hath made everything beautiful in its time." (Ecclesiastes 3:11). These two verses of scripture, when put together, help us see that God works in His own time to maneuver human history into a beautiful end of the story. So, give God time!

Be Courageous

There was a time when generals led the charge into battle. It is said that during World War II, soldiers heard General George Patton yell while charging into battle, "I've read your book, Rommel! I've read your book!" He was referring to "Infantry Attacks" by German Field Marshal Rommel. Patton's courage was bolstered by his intense study of the enemy.

In Israel, living with daily bomb threats has become a part of life. Sirens and alarms ring through the air regularly. If the enemies of Israel can't cross the border, they try to invade the minds of its people. How do the people of Israel handle all this fear-mongering? They resolve to live each day as normal. They go to school, water their gardens, and celebrate birthdays. By choosing to live normal lives amidst constant threats, they declare, "You aren't winning! You must continue living when life is a battle."

Courage only needs a battle to arise. Ironically, your courage is often most apparent when you are concealing your fears. Having courage doesn't mean you are without fear. Rather, courage is the strength to face challenges head-on, especially when you are most afraid. The word 'battle' is defined by Merriam-Webster as "the struggle to succeed or survive." Since the dawn of time, battles have been a part of human history. As long as there are two individuals alive on planet earth, there will be battles, battles of opinions, styles, beliefs. In your lifetime, you will inevitably fight an important battle. Mark it down; at some point along life's journey, you will face an opposing force that insists on stopping you in your tracks. But there is help. Here are a few things you will need:

Intelligence of the enemy.

The adversary is subtle and crafty. "Now the serpent was more crafty than any of the wild animals the LORD God had made." (Genesis 3:1, NIV). In the New Testament, Satan even masquerades as an angel of light. Notice the word "masquerades," which means to disguise oneself or go about disguised. "And no wonder, for Satan himself masquerades as an angel of light;" (2 Corinthians 11:14, AMPC). The enemy often succeeds in hiding his true identity through external means. His greatest influence is working through those unredeemed, manifesting in traits like bitterness, unforgiveness, pride, and jealousy. The spirits against us are, in many instances, more subtle, coming under the guise of fun and adventure.

In the story of the prodigal son, the far country was appealing to his youthfulness. It wasn't Satan directly that appeared, but rather the excitement of a new world. The prodigal was quickly surrounded by opportunistic friends, living life through their fallen nature. To the prodigal, the "far country" seemed attractive, but in the end, it led to his downfall and desertion. He was surrounded by those hoping to capitalize on his money. "There is pleasure in sin for a season." (Hebrews 11:25-26). What started out as exhilarating ended in humiliation. The prodigal was exposed to the cruel world he thought his father sheltered him from. Jesus has the power to expose the schemes of the enemy. There's a lesson in the story of a banker who could spot a fake hundred-dollar bill instantly due to her familiarity with the real thing. Similarly, as we consistently handle the truth, we develop greater awareness of the fake, sharpening our discernment by staying close to the banks of scripture.

A STRATEGY TO ENDURE.

In the Old Testament, Israel faced a physical enemy. In the New Testament, the opposition is more spiritual. For some, victory comes swiftly, but for many, the battle is long and arduous. Jesus has armed us with scripture, prayer, and a vast array of spiritual weapons. "The weapons we fight with are not the weapons of the world. On the contrary, they have divine power to demolish strongholds." (2 Corinthians 10:4, NIV). Often, the lengthy battle is between you and your flesh. Endurance is key to victory. Jesus told the disciples that "he who endures to the end shall be saved." The Greek word for "endures" (hupomeno) refers to fortitude and persistence. We are called to persist in faith; while the battles rage, we can outlast the attack. It may require holding on firmly, but rest assured that our trials have an expiration date.

THE RIGHT MINDSET

The truth is worth fighting for! "Buy the truth, and sell it not; also wisdom, and instruction, and understanding." (Proverbs 23:23, KJV). Once a truth is lost, history records that it is nearly impossible to recover. Unless God intervenes with a revival of absolute truth, years of relativistic thinking are sure to follow. No other nation had such a monopoly on truth as Israel in the Old Testament. Israel was a nation of laws, set apart by absolute truth. If you are to be hated for anything, it will likely be for speaking the truth. During the reign of Josiah, the Old Testament king of Judah, there was a period where the scriptures were lost. In the temple, the sacred law collected dust. What may have been the original writings of Moses sat hidden and abandoned. The result was a nation divided, under attack, and losing influence in the world. The absence of law leads to devastating depravity. The leaders of Israel were tasked with keeping truth before the nation to ensure spiritual health. Every seven years, the law of Moses was to be read, leading to a sobering effect and a refreshing change in the land. We must awaken the pulpits for an authentic revival of the Bible.

"And Moses commanded them, saying, At the end of every seven years, in the solemnity of the year of release, in the feast of tabernacles, When all Israel is come to appear before the LORD thy God in the place which he shall choose, thou shalt read this law before all Israel in their hearing. Gather the people together, men and women, and children, and thy stranger that is within thy gates, that they may hear, and that they may learn, and fear the LORD your God, and observe to do all the words of this law: And that their children, which have not known anything, may hear, and learn to fear the LORD your God, as long as ye live in the land whither ye go over Jordan to possess it." (Deuteronomy 31:10-13, KJV). All generations were represented in the reading of the scriptures. Truth must be passed down from our mothers and fathers to the hearts of our children. If we lose our pulpits, it will reflect in the polls and, most importantly, in the family. A loss of morals in the community indicates that truth has been neglected and godly fear abandoned. Disregard for human life signifies a slighted fear of God. The law is designed to keep godly convictions alive. The battle for absolute truth is the single most important battle in your life.

Courage

Goliath would never have fallen if David had lacked courage. Samson pushed down the pillars without eyes, but not without courage. It takes courage to defeat your enemies. For the believer, courage is the offspring of faith. Every breakthrough lies just on the other side of the courage to follow through.

Lessons From David
Beware of Idle Time

"And it came to pass, after the year had expired, at the time when kings go forth to battle, that David sent Joab, and his servants with him, and all Israel; and they destroyed the children of Ammon, and besieged Rabbah. But David tarried still at Jerusalem. And it came to pass in an eveningtide, that David arose from off his bed, and walked upon the roof of the king's house: and from the roof he saw a woman washing herself; and the woman was very beautiful to look upon." (2 Samuel 11:1-2, KJV).

David, better known as the "Giant Killer," was an accomplished soldier. Throughout most of David's biblical narrative, he is engaged in some form of battle. One day it's against a bear or a lion, the next it's the giant Goliath. However, in 2 Samuel 11:1-2, we find David in a rare moment of ease. He stayed home during the optimal fighting season. Perhaps the battles had become routine for the king of Israel. Maybe David had fought his share. If anyone deserved a break, it was him, and his title and position afforded him that luxury. David was the king, after all.

Fighting battles was second nature to David. He thrived when there was an enemy to conquer. In 2 Samuel chapter 11, a different kind of battle arises in David's life the battle of temptation. He doesn't flee from it and ultimately pays the consequences. Why did he succumb to this temptation? We are not explicitly told, but there are some possibilities to consider. David was not actively in-

Lessons From David

volved in leading battles, which was dangerous for him. The lesson here is that there is always something worth fighting for. If only King David had channeled his energy into a new song or psalm, he might have avoided this dark chapter of his life. David needed to find new battlefields to engage in. Similarly, our enemies will not always be the same.

I personally dislike battles of any kind, but I acknowledge that there is always something worth fighting for, such as truth, freedom, and the rights of the unborn. It's often said, "All it takes for evil to prevail is for good men to do nothing." Beware of the dangers of idle time. Never forget that "the battle belongs to the Lord." All of them! Take time today; there is a battle that demands your presence.

"David needed to change his battlefields. Like David's story, enemies will not always be the same."

THE DANGER OF A COMPLIMENT

"So the women sang as they danced, and said: 'Saul has slain his thousands, And David his ten thousands'" (1 Samuel 18:7 NKJV).

David, a champion and decorated leader, held the number one leadership skill—the power to influence. This earned him no shortage of followers. His aura was one of victory! He was the friend everyone wanted by their side in times of trouble. David's fighting record was impressive:

- David vs. the bear? Won by David
- David vs. the lion? Won by David
- David vs. Goliath? Won by David
- David vs. Saul's jealousy? Won by David
- David vs. a compliment?

Can a compliment be dangerous? Absolutely. Living for compliments can ruin even the best among us. It's a significant danger for any leader, the mistake of being overly occupied with one's successes. Unproven and immature leadership can often be driven more by applause than inspiration. First, be wary of the trap of trying to exceed a previous compliment. Secondly, be thankful when your gifts and talents are acknowledged. A compliment sown is a gift to the soul, providing stamina for the journey and a restful reward for everyday labors. There's nothing inherently evil about a word timely spoken. Phrases like "Don't give up," "Great

Lessons From David

job," or "I am impressed," have sparked much good. However, should flattery come your way, it's crucial to stay alert, especially when basking in the glow of life's proverbial mountaintops. Keep it all in perspective. Remember, we are not that good; only God is!

I might be off base here, but what if that song sung by the dancing young ladies—"Saul has slain his thousands but David his ten thousands"—was David's biggest battle? That's a lot for a young man to process. Success is rewarding but must be viewed in perspective. David fought many fierce fights, but this might have been his toughest. We are no different. Like David, we face dreaded internal battles, wars no one else knows about. The key? Remind yourself, "I am blessed, but to God be the glory." Practice redirecting all praise to Him. "I won because I simply obeyed what He asked of me." That's the way to keep winning! And yes, I believe David won that battle, but it surely wasn't his easiest.

"Unproven and immature leadership can often be driven by applause instead of inspiration."

A Campaign of Kindness

Just like that! David, once a shepherd boy, is crowned king over all Israel. But that phrase "just like that" doesn't quite capture the truth. David's journey to the throne was long and arduous, filled with "many dangers, toils, and snares," as the famous hymn by John Newton goes. It's often the case that the longer the journey, the greater the appreciation. "The harder the climb, the more rewarding the view!" Why? Because appreciation is directly linked to investment. The more time and labor we put into something, the more we value it.

David's first few years as king were bustling with activity. He was continually adjusting his crown, symbolizing the myriad tasks he accomplished: bringing the ark of the covenant back to Israel, recovering their national treasure; securing Jerusalem from the Jebusites; and establishing it as the city of the "Great King." Finally, David sits down, taking a moment to reflect. A quick mental survey and he realizes, "I did not get here alone." He remembers a specific friend who loved him long before he was king Jonathan. They had made a serious covenant, a blood covenant, signified by a scar on David's hand. "When we arrive wherever God takes us, we will remember this day."

The ivory throne of the palace feels so right, yet David can't fully enjoy it. Something doesn't fit; there are loose ends, important matters left unfinished. His next campaign is one of kindness. Despite having been a victim of Saul's abuse of power, maturity borne from struggle has blessed David with a heart for others. In an exemplary display of this character, David asks one of the most profound questions in the Bible: "Who can I bless, from the house of Saul today?" This question reflects his deep sense of gratitude and resolve to give back. Now in a position of great authority, David chooses to rule with integrity and mercy. One of the true measures of a leader is how they handle power. The question remains, "when you come into power, whatever that may mean for you, will you rule with mercy, or will you rule with fear?" I pray that you choose kindness.

"One of the great measures of a leader is how he handles power."

The Lord is my Shepherd

"The LORD is my shepherd; I shall not want. He makes me lie down in green pastures." (Psalm 23:1-2).

Viewing life as a journey enriches our understanding of its complexities and beauties. This journey of life takes us through a myriad of experiences—forward towards new horizons and challenges, sometimes back to familiar beginnings, and often in circles that teach us lessons we might have missed the first time. On this journey, we encounter discouragements, delays, and detours. If life were a highway, it would undoubtedly be a fast-paced one, where moments pass swiftly and challenges come at us relentlessly.

Life is seldom neat and tidy. In Psalm 23, we are reminded that life is more akin to a journey or a hike, filled with varying terrains—from lush pastures to daunting mountains. This journey is replete with ascents and descents, with each bump providing an opportunity to grip and climb higher. The very obstacles that seem to hinder us can become the stepping stones we need for progress. A rock climber finds their way upward by using the ledges in the rock; similarly, we navigate life's challenges by leveraging our experiences and learning from them.

Psalm 23 serves as a guide through life's treacherous and beautiful paths. It is a testament for those transitioning from breakdown to blessing, from attack to victory. It speaks to all who are navigating the tumultuous yet rewarding journey of life. This Psalm, penned by David in retrospect, reflects on the many roles God played in his life, chief among them being a faithful tour guide who never abandons us.

Here is what I have learned about the Lord, my Shepherd:

- He guides me towards what is best for me, even when I am unaware.
- His love for me surpasses any other; it is deep, unconditional, and everlasting.
- In His devotion, He would lay down His life for me, as He has already demonstrated.
- He leads me to places where growth and development are inevitable.
- In the darkest paths of my life, He sees clearly and guides me with precision.
- No matter how far I wander, His pursuit is relentless, and His recovery, certain.

Such is the nature of a good Shepherd; always guiding, always loving, always present.

> *"He will never lead you anywhere you cannot grow."*

Giants Still Fall

"Goliath stood and shouted to the ranks of Israel, 'Why do you come out and line up for battle?'" (1 Samuel 17:8 NIV).

At the edge of the road stood a daunting young man, shirtless and swinging wooden nunchucks, his muscles flexing in an apparent attempt to intimidate and bully two younger boys. His challenge? A confrontation on the road. This all began because two boys fancied the same girl, my cousin and this muscular adversary. This was my initial brush with what I perceived as a 'giant.'

In a somewhat naive attempt at diplomacy, I approached him, hoping to diffuse the situation by saying, "We don't want any trouble." His response was a gentle tap on my face, igniting the situation. Just then, my cousin's father emerged from the house, his stern words causing the bully to flee. An elder, who had been vigilantly watching from afar, saved me from further embarrassment.

The saga of David is incomplete without the mention of his confrontation with a giant, Goliath. Unlike the bully in my story, Goliath's intimidation tactics weren't just physical presence and bravado; they included his towering stature, his booming voice, and his formidable weapons. Yet, when David heard Goliath's taunts, he was filled with a youthful courage, questioning the Israelites' passive stance against this Philistine. David's strength came not from physical prowess but from a life where everything was hard-earned. From a tender age, isolated with his flock, David learned to be independent, resourceful, and, above all, deeply connected with God.

Instructed by God, David selected five smooth stones from the riverbed, perhaps with a premonition that one was destined for Goliath. David understood that when confronting a giant, one must be proactive and face the challenge head-on. He didn't cower but ran towards Goliath and, with his practiced sling skills and divine aid, brought the giant tumbling down.

My own experience with the 'giant' was different. I tried to reason, only to find that sometimes, confrontation requires a different kind of intervention. Today, we have Jesus, our vigilant guardian, watching over us. He imparts the courage and assertiveness we need. Remember, you are never truly alone. If need be, Jesus will step in to fend off your giants.

> *"Don't hide from your giant, or he only gets bigger."*

DAVID AND THE GIANT

"Reaching into his bag and taking out a stone, he slung it and struck the Philistine on the forehead. The stone sank into his forehead, and he fell face-down on the ground." (1 Samuel 17:49 NIV).

Giants are real, and we have all encountered them. They often appear as immovable objects that stand in our way, chanting phrases like "You have no chance," and "I dare you." Their taunts can be relentless: "Why? Who do you think you are?" and "Where is your God now?" They question our capabilities: "They won't hire you; where is your degree? What qualifications can you possibly have?"

David faced a literal giant, Goliath, who stood nine feet tall. Consider your own giants. Are they named lack, fear of trust, or insecurity about your appearance or financial status? Perhaps you feel it's always "A day late and a dollar short." Everyone has a giant, something that makes us feel small, insignificant, and inadequate.

David wasn't physically imposing. Saul's armor didn't fit him. Saul was the people's choice, but David was God's pick. Being chosen by God is what truly matters. He sees you in your moments of despair and still loves you when you make mistakes. David's story teaches us that while mentors, teachers, and heroes are valuable, the pressure to measure up to them can be overwhelming. Be who God called you to be. David relied on what he knew—a sling and stones. He valued simplicity and was unafraid to rely on what was effective rather than what was popular or new.

We love underdog stories, and so does God. When the odds are against us, it's an opportunity for God to show His might. Shed the weight of others' expectations and be authentic before God. David used simple tools: stones, a shepherd's bag, and a sling. Stones are often found in valleys; perhaps that's where you are meant to find your weapons. You will encounter many giants on your journey, but remember, there will always be more stones than giants, more victories than defeats, and more reasons for gratitude than sorrow.

Face your giant head-on. Let your prayers be your sling, and remember that Jesus has already fought for us. When you confront your giants, take them to Calvary's hill—that's where the ultimate battle is won.

Prayer Focus

Father, in Jesus' name, we lay all our giants before you. We are grateful for the compliments we receive, but we acknowledge that all glory belongs to you. Deliver us from our temptations and rescue us from moments of dangerous inactivity. Inspire in our hearts melodies of praise. We recognize that jealousy can lead to much harm; help us to keep our eyes firmly fixed on you. We pray for your peace to envelop our lives today. Amen.

> *"There will be many giants in the way where you are trying to go, but there will always be more stones than giants!"*

Lessons from Peter

Behold

"Simon, Simon, behold, Satan demanded to have you, that he might sift you like wheat, but I have prayed for you that your faith may not fail. And when you have turned again, strengthen your brothers." (Luke 22:31-32).

These verses in Luke contain profound insights into spiritual warfare. Jesus' words to Peter, "Simon, Simon, behold, Satan has demanded you," serve as a stark warning of an impending attack. Remarkably, Jesus doesn't rebuke Satan or halt the demand; instead, He acknowledges it, signifying that Satan has limits imposed upon him.

Satan's intent is clear: to sift Peter. Sifting is distinct from a straightforward attack. An attack seeks to overpower and obliterate, akin to a violent tornado devastating all in its path. It leaves victims bewildered, exclaiming, "The calamity came suddenly!" "Destruction was swift!" "We never thought it would happen to us!" Attacks evoke emotional turmoil.

Sifting, on the other hand, involves a meticulous separation, a gradual and sequential attrition. It entails the painful removal of what is unnecessary. Peter, in this sifting process, would grapple with his emotions, and his resolve to stand firm would be severely tested. Simon would face relentless mental assaults, and while the temptation to give in might seem absurd, he would succumb. His moral frailty would be exposed. This is a shared human experience. Under intense pressure, our belief systems and realities are either solidified or relinquished. Satan's goal was to shatter Peter's character, convincing him that his errors and failures disqualified him from divine purpose.

However, Jesus provides the key to victory in a single word: "Behold." While it may not appear revelatory at first, it holds profound significance. "Behold" means "to gaze" or "observe with vision." It invites us to see what is transpiring. In times of sifting, we are urged to pause, observe, and recognize that something remarkable is unfolding. This word, frequently used in Scripture, hints at preparation, getting ready to witness God working wonders. God is at work, and what is He doing? He is holding you in prayer. This is a beautiful image: God praying on your behalf. He is advocating for you. Just as Peter needed a vision of an interceding Savior, so do we. Behold the Lord today. He is fighting for you. Slow down, "be still and know that He is God." He is praying for you.

> *"While under such intense pressures, our belief structures and realities are either tethered to or let go."*

"That Your Faith May Not Fail"

"Simon, Simon, Satan has asked to sift each of you like wheat. But I have pleaded in prayer for you, Simon, that your faith should not fail. So when you have repented and turned to me again, strengthen your brothers." (Luke 22:31-32, NLT).

"Faith is often the child of fear." Peter's faith was so strong that it gained him notoriety among his peers. Without a vote cast among the young fishermen, Simon took the lead. No doubt about it, he earned it, at least somewhat. In a relentless flash of courage, Simon walked on water. Who else in the disciples' group walked on a wave or two? Zero, zilch, only Peter.

It all began one stormy night as he threw his courage over the side of the fishing boat and exited onto a curling wave. In the face of whipping winds, Peter defied nature and walked to Jesus. Peter didn't sink, not until his faith took a dip. After a few steps in faith, Simon made a scene. His voice changed pitch, Peter lost his focus. In the blowing rain, he lost sight of Jesus. The walk of faith was over quickly. When we lose sight of Jesus, life sinks

Jesus was walking on water. What a benchmark. Jesus set the bar high. I give it to Peter here; he had this part right, he wanted to imitate Jesus. Shouldn't we all? Outside of the transfiguration and the resurrection appearances, there may not be a greater display of Jesus in power. As long as Peter stayed focused, he succeeded. When he did not— you know the rest of the story! Fast forward from the storm on Galilee to hours before Jesus goes through his suffering. Jesus is held captive. Temple guards hold him fast. Soon Roman soldiers will too. Peter is in a storm again, this time a storm brewing in his heart. He can't believe that the one who walked in the storm is now heading to a cruel Cross. He wants the water-walking Jesus but not the cross-carrying Jesus. Peter is drowning in his own cowardice.

In Luke 22:31, we are told Jesus prayed that Peter's faith may not "fail".. the word "FAIL" in the original language is where we get the word eclipse. That describes Simon at that precise moment. Simon's faith was hidden. That is what an eclipse does. It hides the light. Peter had a total eclipse of faith. He hid! Much of spiritual warfare arises because we tend to succeed where Jesus is popular—church, Bible study groups. But it's the unpopular or unappreciated Jesus that we hide from. We all know there are many places that no longer welcome Jesus with open arms anymore. Those are the challenges to shine.

Jesus doesn't give up on Peter; rather, the Gospel tells us Jesus prayed knowing this very day would come. He prayed for him to be converted, restored, just like nothing ever happened. Soon after Simon's failure, there is a moment in all of this where Jesus' eyes meet Peter's. I believe Jesus held Peter in the eyes of love. That's key to victory in our spiritual battles. Jesus loves to save us, and most of the time it's from our own undoing. He knows when these days will come. Be reminded he prayed for you before the bad days. Before the failure, he had already prayed. May God help you today find the courage to follow Jesus in the unpopular moments as much as in the popular ones.

> *"May God help you today find the courage to follow Jesus in the unpopular moments as much as in the popular ones."*

WHEN YOU TURN BACK

"But I have prayed for you that your faith may not fail. And you, when you have turned back, strengthen your brothers." (Luke 22:32 NLT).

We have all said it, "If I ever get another chance, I will do things differently next time." For Peter, he has become infatuated with the thought of redeeming himself. In his mind, the rooster's crow still rings, and his betrayal of Jesus still stings. Yet, he will have to wait.

For nearly three years, Peter had not been able to hide it. His personal agenda crowded out and disabled any close relationships. He had dreams; big dreams. Dreams of a throne, a crown, and to finish first in apostolic succession. He is a hierarchical thinker. The thought of answering other people's questions would make him feel important. "In charge has a nice ring to it," thought Peter. He is intoxicated with power. We may never know why. Is he hot-tempered? Does he seek accomplishment because of self-esteem issues? Possibly. Only heaven knows. Like Peter before his fall, many of us at one time or another have sought recognition. We daydream of a life filled with grand finishes. The truth is, that's not realistic or in the will of heaven.

Peter needs a map to get back to where he was before he ran away. Jesus said when you "turn back" or, as one translation puts it, "when you recover, strengthen your brethren." Those words are his way back home. Peter will get redemption. He will have an opportunity to redeem himself. Thankfully, the regret will disappear. When will it begin? It's right there hidden in the words of Jesus. "When you are converted," "turned back strengthen your brethren."

The fall of Peter happened as he was chasing titles and building his legacy. Peter, the "storm chaser," Peter, "the security guard" (as if Jesus needed one), "the right-hand man of the Messiah." Peter was in love with accolades.

The first step to redemption for Peter was to "turn back" in the direction of all those he stepped on and over. Here is what he learned: Great warfare arrives on our doorsteps when we forget we are called to serve one another. Remember, Jesus said things like we are "the body," "the assembly," saying we are interconnected. We need one another. Peter will triumph when he turns back and realizes "people" are God's priority. Make it your priority.

Did Peter make it home? The answer is found in his epistles. You be the judge. Peter writes later, "..and godliness with brotherly affection, and brotherly affection with love. For if these qualities are yours and are increasing, they keep you from being ineffective or unfruitful in the knowledge of our Lord Jesus Christ. For whoever lacks these qualities is so nearsighted that he is blind, having forgotten that he was cleansed from his former sins" (2 Peter 1:6-9, NLT). Amen. I say he figured it out.!

> "Great warfare arrives on our doorsteps when we forget we are called to serve one another."

The Time of Testing

"Peter said to him, 'Lord, I am ready to go with you both to prison and to death.' Jesus said, 'I tell you, Peter, the rooster will not crow this day, until you deny three times that you know me.'" (Luke 22:33-34 ESV).

It was my least favorite day in school: Test day. Even more sinister was the pop quiz day! You had to love it when the teacher announced, "Close your books, class; today is pop quiz day." It probably needs no explanation, but just in case, a quiz is a short test (normally) that you are unprepared for and probably are going to fail. Why? It's simple, you aren't ready. Test days are different in that it is not the unpreparedness that gets you, it's the pressure.

Pressure! It is what makes the ocean pearl a jewel. It's what forms diamonds out of organic material buried deep in the earth. Pressure treatment is what renders wood impervious to weathering. Pressure somehow creates longevity. Pressure has the ability to make things costly.

Then there is Peter! He has just let the prophetic words of Jesus glance off his hearing. In one ear and out the other, "Simon, when you are converted, did you hear me, Simon? The rooster will crow after you deny me three times." Jesus could not have put it more succinctly. Peter's response is classic Peter: "Oh Jesus, you know.. I will follow you anywhere.. I'll even go as far as dying for you."

Within a few hours, Peter will behave in a way he is not accustomed to. He will follow Jesus at a distance. The temple guards close the door tight. A few guards stay outside. While behind closed doors, the high priest sits with questions already premeditated. "Who are you?" The pressure in that room must have reached maximum overload. Jesus is wedged between religious heavyweights and unseen dark principalities. Everyone involved is hoping that he fails. Quite the contrary. Jesus doesn't flinch. He says all the right words. He is poised, composed, and confident! The one who created the oceans and carved the valleys aces the exam. Jesus demonstrated for us what it means to be calm in chaos. He is Jesus. Pressure he understands. He has dealt with it all His life. Pressure to perform. The pressure to fulfill expectations. Part of his dualistic nature is that He became like us, flesh and blood. Why is that important? His victories are very real. Don't forget that!

It is Peter's turn. The Peter who said, "I'll follow you anywhere," stopped several feet from the door. A few fierce-looking soldiers had something to do with that, I am sure. Following Jesus can lead us into some uncomfortable straits. Peter is tested. The word "temptation" in the Greek language, I am told, can mean "to pierce," as in "to pierce to see what comes out." What Peter teaches us is that the test reveals what is on the inside of our hearts. If fear is in there, it will come out under a test.

Peter is everything but grace under pressure. The truth is we all would have run away. Gracefully, Jesus allows us the opportunity to retake some tests. Peter denied three times, yet in John's gospel, Jesus asked Peter three times "to feed my sheep." Peter gets another test day. What the test did for Peter is of great value. Peter becomes a Pearl. Peter has developed costly faith. The pressure has made him more attentive. He slows down and listens. He becomes a man who leans on the Lord heavily. What can we learn from this? A test informs you and me of what is on the inside. There is an old saying you may have heard, "if you can't stand the heat, then get out of the kitchen." Let us grow in grace as we stand in the "fiery trials." May the God who has never lost a battle strengthen you in the fight!

PRAYER FOCUS

Our heavenly Father, in Jesus' name, I pray that you will strengthen me today should I face a culture that doesn't welcome you. May I open doors today for your grace to step in. Father, help us lean on you when we are under attack. We patiently wait while you fight our battles. We trust in your faithfulness, not ours. We do not trust in our character, only yours. We do not trust in our sufficiency, only yours. Let us behold your perfect faithfulness in every struggle. Amen..

> *"The test reveals what is on the inside of our hearts."*

Lessons From Joseph

Joseph and the All-Season Coat

"Israel loved Joseph more than any of his other sons because he was the child of his old age. And he made him an elaborately embroidered coat. When his brothers realized that their father loved him more than them, they grew to hate him—they wouldn't even speak to him." (Genesis 37:3-4).

"Through sunshine and rain, laughter and pain, His promises for me stay the same. Oh, what a blessing I have found resting in his well-designed plan. When I don't understand, I hold tight to his hand, and God never makes a mistake." It is one of my dad's favorite songs. Mine too. A true depiction of life.

Every day is not always filled with bright sunny skies. There are some clouds that will hang low. There will be days filled with bad news, days you win, followed up by losses. Stormy days, dark days—this list could exhaust you, but you get it. Life has no guarantees. If there is one, expect the unexpected.

Jacob loved his youngest son Joseph in a special way. Joseph was the benefactor of a father who had learned from his mistakes. Jacob would heap all those years of what he "should have done" upon Joseph. Jacob made Joseph an all-season coat. One study suggested that the material used for the coat had the ability to keep you warm in the winter and cool in the summer. Its spectacular array of colors solidified Joseph's confidence. There is a message from a father to a son in that coat. "My Son, there will be sunshine and rain, laughter and pain." But let this coat encourage you. Be reminded that seasons will change. People will change, you will change. This coat is a reminder that as the seasons change, your father's love will never change. It will always protect you in every season of your life. God is immutable. His character will never change. He will cover you like Joseph's coat of many colors.

> *"This coat is a reminder that as the seasons change, your father's love will never change."*

12

NOT EVERYONE WILL LIKE YOU!

"When his brothers realized that their father loved him more than them, they grew to hate him—they wouldn't even speak to him." (Genesis 37:4 MSG).

She was innocent, gullible, and vulnerable. The she? My daughter's adorable new puppy. Daisy was a four-month-old Golden-doodle, now the new puppy on the block. She paid me a surprise visit. Unfortunately, the surprise was on her. If a dog ever was smiling, she was from ear to ear that day. Daisy, full of puppy energy, came running towards me, excited and ready to introduce herself. She only reached about halfway across the living room floor when it happened. My eight-year-old Molly, "about half her size" Pekingese, leaped on her back and reminded Daisy that this is my house! The rest of the night I watched as little Daisy lost the bounce in her step. She looked cautiously around every corner, showing concern with every step. For the first time in her young life, she learned the inevitable in the dog world: that "not everyone is going to like you!"

Human life is much the same. The quicker we learn we are not everyone's "cup of tea," the quicker we can get on with our happiness. Joseph has a high calling. The beautiful coat was his promise of a favored life. It attracted more than compliments; it attracted jealousies. Where there is jealousy, there is fear. His brothers feared that Joseph would finish first, that Joseph would carry home trophies to their second-place ribbons. Afraid that Joseph would remind them, "Dad made me this coat!" The brothers were all afraid he would inherit patriarchal blessings. Jealousy is bad, pure and simple. Joseph, like Jesus, endured the spears of jealousy.

What do we do when we are not the favorite? Would we attack preemptively? Might we lash out inappropriately? Maybe we would find a big pit and bury someone's dream like Joseph's brothers did. Joseph too was the new kid on the block, at home, in Egypt—everywhere he went, attacks followed. When reading Joseph's story, you get the feeling he never lost that smile. Joseph kept his energy. For Joseph, a lifetime of wounds generated the ability to forgive. Finally, his tears turned to laughter as he was reunited with his family. In Egypt, he would smile again. The jailer hears him say, "Hello, I am Joseph." To the Pharaoh, "Hi, my name is Joseph." Be like Joseph, never lose your smile! Even in the presence of your enemies, show your smile! "For love will cover a multitude of sins.""

> *"Where there is jealousy, there is fear."*

Joseph Had a Dream

Martin Luther King Jr. is one of America's foremost historical figures. Many overlook the fact that Dr. King was a superb pulpit minister. His sermons were articulate, scriptural, and fruitful. He was his generation's voice in the wilderness. One night, while under a divine hand, Dr. King shared a message that had prophetic implications. At some point, he had been to the mountaintop and was given a vision of the future. His dream has, with every passing year, proven accurate. As Dr. King walked with the Lord, he was given a dream so big that it triggered haters.

Joseph in the Bible story is similar. Joseph's brothers attempted murder because of this young man's dreams. Dreams are evidence that God is already present in our tomorrows. God is not bound by time. He transcends time. He sees the entirety of human history in one glance. He goes before us to prepare the way. A dream is not only the evidence of an eternal God; a dream is the painting of God on our mental canvas. As God transcends time, he takes in all that is happening at once and drops hints, clues, and warnings into our spirits. Getting right down to it, God believes in you so much that he has big dreams for you. Joseph was a dreamer.

The dreams Joseph experienced were big—dreams about the stars, the moon, and solar systems. That's how expansive Joseph's dreams were to become. Joseph's future leadership would change the outcome of human history. In the movie "Schindler's List," an old Jewish parable is shared: "He who saves one life saves the world entirely." Joseph was to Egypt and the surrounding nations a savior. Joseph, being forewarned by a dream, helped put together a plan to survive a severe famine. Egypt survived—Israel survived. What do we trace the survival to? The one night Joseph dreamed. He dreamed of leadership. He dreamed of a famine. Joseph had dreams. God wants you to know we still live in a world where people are in famine. Where we are in great need of spiritual and moral leadership. What has God shown you in his plan to save the world? God has a dream just for you. My prayer is "may you dream big again!""

> *"Dreams are evidence that God is already present in our tomorrows."*

14

A NIGHT IN A PIT

"Then they took him and cast him into a pit. And the pit was empty; there was no water in it." (Genesis 37:24).

So you paid too much for the used car. We've all done it—failed to do the proper research. Like Eve, you bit into the apple! The shiny cover got you. It feels awful, but at least it's not a night's stay in a dry and deep pit. You trusted them with the secret, but somehow it got out that you have been struggling financially. Your pride takes a severe blow. That's hurtful, humiliating, but it's not as bad as a dark pit. Pits have crawly creatures in them. Pits are claustrophobia at its worst. Pits represent life's lowest moments.

Joseph was cast into a pit. Not just a bad day. A pit. Not in an argument with a spouse or neighbor; something far worse is a real-life pit. A pit has no food, no water, no hope. That's what that pit was designed to do—break Joseph's hope. That would have only been possible if Joseph had not known God. But he did! He knew that he was not alone. Oh no, the pit was very empty, but empty isn't the same as alone. You can be empty in your life. Empty in your outlook, empty in joy. Empty on finance and fun. Empty, empty, empty, but with Christ, you are never alone. Here is what Joseph learned in the pit: "when my mother and father forsake me," God never will. What he learned at the intersection of trust and being alone is invaluable. It isn't until you have no one else in whom to trust that many times we find God standing somewhere in the shadows.

If you feel isolated, alone, and are in a dark place in your life, just wait—God will show up. It may not be the way you thought. But He will never leave or forsake you. The Bible says that God is an "ever-present help in the time of trouble." When Joseph arrived in Egypt, perhaps they asked him, "Where are you from, Joseph?" I kind of imagine he said something like, "oh, nowhere famous really, just a hole in the ground!"

PRAYER FOCUS

Our heavenly Father, we thank you for the robes of righteousness you cover us with. Lord, I don't always appreciate the pits of life, but I know they are working out your plan. Father, my coat may be torn, but my faith and integrity are intact. Father, let me focus on the dream and not the insults or the past. In both famines of heart and life, I am reminded you are my source. May truth reign in my life and throughout your kingdom. My Savior, may I possess the gifts you have given me in humility. Father, what the enemy has meant for evil, I put into your hands now; you will do what's right. In Jesus' name, we ask, Amen.

> *"It isn't until you have no one else in whom to trust that many times we find God standing somewhere in the shadows."*

Lessons From Nehemiah

You Have to Start Somewhere

"And so I arrived in Jerusalem. After I had been there for three days, I got up in the middle of the night, I and a few men who were with me." (Nehemiah 2:11).

A maintenance man is not in high demand until something is broken. A factory running smoothly is an orchestra of pings and screeches, whistles, and whines. When these go silent, the first person called in is the repairman. Nehemiah was the Lord's repairman.

Nehemiah shows up in Jerusalem to survey the damage. What once resembled gates now lay propped up against the stone walls. This is discouraging compared to the king's palace he had just left. The city walls are damaged and not in use.

Meanwhile, Nehemiah is enjoying some amenities with a king. Nehemiah's job title is cupbearer to the king, a highly trusted position. The job location is the palace in Shushan. Shushan is palatial, living at its finest. If you want to be out of touch with the common man, a king's house is a pretty good place for that to happen.

While enjoying the fine life, a visiting entourage from Jerusalem bears Nehemiah the bad news: Jerusalem is in a sad state. The capital city lay broken, unfinished, and dangerous. Their pleas for help touched Nehemiah deeply. Nehemiah shows up at Jerusalem

Lessons From Nehemiah

with a heart that resembles the gates and walls, broken. His plan? Take a walk and figure out just where to start.

Nehemiah had the king's approval. More importantly, Nehemiah had the favor of God. Nehemiah now just needed to know where to start, where to begin. So often when areas of neglect and brokenness arise, the greatest challenge is, "Where do I start?" In comparison to Nehemiah's story, we can know for certain that God has commissioned our steps. And be sure that He has blessed and opened every door possible. But there are always many unknowns and challenges that we face. Nehemiah had them, and we will too. Ever notice God doesn't always give us all the instructions? If He did, our task wouldn't be by faith. Just because we have approval and opportunity doesn't always make it easy.

Nehemiah did not take a walk looking for sympathy but the right starting point. He was processing a plan on where to begin. Next time you feel overwhelmed, and the "to-do list" seems to never end, start by taking a "Nehemiah walk." Boldly look at the destruction and declare the word of the Lord. It is in the broken-down places where you find God has a plan. God gave Ezekiel a plan while in a valley of dry bones, basically a cemetery. God showed Jeremiah where to begin in a potter's field— the pottery graveyard. He can show you where to start putting the pieces back together, no matter how scattered they may be. *Don't forget that every finish line had a starting line.

"

"It is in the broken-down places where you find God has a plan."

LOOSE LIPS SINK SHIPS

"I got up in the middle of the night, I and a few men who were with me. I hadn't told anyone what my God had put in my heart to do for Jerusalem." (Nehemiah 2:11 NIV).

During World War II, keeping information was critical for winning the war. The slogan "loose lips sink ships" began rolling off government printing presses, all in the effort to stay a step ahead of the enemy. The enemy was looking for any advantage possible in the effort to steal our language codes.

Nehemiah waded into the night air on horseback, reaching outside the protective walls of the city. The path tightened to where he could only pass on foot. For a better view, he had to look into the valley; looking up the valley, he got a good picture of how bad things were. It all happened at night when Nehemiah couldn't sleep. There are times in your life where sleep will escape you. At first, it seems as if it is a natural occurrence. But, in reality, these are strategic times where God wakes us up because He is about to work undercover.

We learn that Nehemiah did not want a crowd. He was aware there was opposition inside the city. There will always be those who can't stand to see success in and around your life. Be careful who you share your dreams with. The work we do in private will solidify our strengths and success. In other words, keep quiet! Keep working.

Celebration will come in just fifty-two days, but for now, Jerusalem's rebuild needs momentum. Nehemiah wants to move as secretly as possible until the strength and structure are too far along for the enemy to stop. Nehemiah has one of the defining qualities of a leader: he has vision. "The ability to see the finish line way before the starting block." Visionaries have eagle-eyed precision, a gift to see the finished results while still in the embryonic stages. For Nehemiah, he had to deflect the disorder and visualize swinging gates and strong walls.

Nehemiah did not tell anyone what the Lord had put in his heart. Thieves steal what we often keep unlocked. Nehemiah locked up in his heart the plans the Lord gave him. Why? Unfortunately, in spiritual warfare, we never know who the adversary may use undercover. So it is best to be still and trust God. Keep your words between you and the Lord. "Loose lips still sink ships."

> *"Be careful who you share your dreams with."*

Troublesome Times

"The street shall be built again, and the wall, even in troublous times." (Daniel 9:25 KJV).

In the last year (2023), we have witnessed record high inflation. The housing market has felt the headwinds of overpriced listings. Wall Street is as stable as water. The workforce shortage is taking a toll on everyone's patience. In a few words, people are angry, distraught, and fearful. The last thing you would think to do is build, right? This financial climate isn't very conducive to productivity. More of a financial freeze is in order. At times such news can be so discouraging we can't find the hope to pray. It was a very similar economy Nehemiah was facing when God told him to rebuild the walls and gates of Jerusalem. In my years of serving in ministry and the business world, I have learned a few things that happen in troublesome times.

Separation happens.

Weak companies don't survive weak markets. It lends to retooling and competition which helps the economy pick up steam. Nehemiah was rebuilding the walls and retooling a struggling society.

Relocation happens.

Trouble moves people. In the story of Ruth, a famine moved them. She is in the lineage of the Messiah. What if she never relocated? Trouble moves people to where they are needed.

Galvanization happens.

They all had a mind to work. That doesn't happen often. A common enemy brings uncommon camaraderie.

Opportunity happens.

Solomon said, "If we regard the wind we will never sow.." (Ecclesiastes 11:4). Isaac sowed in famine, he reaped a hundredfold. There is no better time to start something than in troubled times. God honors that kind of faith.

Nehemiah was exemplary in troublesome times. He was the rebuilder of life's broken-down walls. Walls denote security in the book of Nehemiah. The repairing of the walls of Jerusalem was a team effort. There will come a time when trouble will surround you on every hand. Your faith will seem distant. The enemy will whisper "I have got you." Your heart will race, your breathing will quicken, but don't quit. Lay there! Stand there! Go forward in faith. Keep building. What I have learned is you can build and finish what you started even in times of trouble. But, you must not go it alone. Find a prayer partner. Humble yourself under the hands of the Almighty God, get some help. Don't quit; troublesome times can be your most productive times.

> "There is no better time to start something than in troubled times. God honors that kind of faith."

A Mind to Work

"So we built the wall, and the entire wall was joined together up to half its height, for the people had a mind to work." (Nehemiah 4:6).

The sound of a symphony is, well, complex. The orchestra is the "Einstein" of music. The details are accentuated. The power notes are punctuated. The flow is melodious to the ear. In the western world, we are more familiar with solo artists and four-piece bands than an orchestra. The beauty of an orchestra lies in the unity of the group. An orchestra is a collaboration of talents and interpretations coming together for one message!

Here is one truth that Nehemiah can teach us: There are several ways to get a group to join a noble cause. But none greater than a common foe. In the book of Nehemiah, the enemy uses insults and mockery in an attempt to dishearten the building project. Sanballat and Tobias were jealous adversaries and wouldn't stop short of anything to halt progress. The insults only served to galvanize the Jewish workers. The people had a "mind to work."

Have you noticed one of the common attempts of Satan is to do the opposite? He wants to get our minds to work on everything but "the good work." He wants us to work overtime worrying. He wants you to work hard on being selfish. To isolate you from the team, the body of Christ, or the church. He strategizes to scatter.

The people of Jerusalem combated the threats with a symphony of togetherness, knowing that God would conduct a masterpiece. One of the seasons Solomon wrote about was a season to build. When you are criticized and laughed at—keep working. Take up company with like-minded workers. Nothing the enemy hates worse than unity. Why? The safest place for you is in a place of unity. In the book of Acts, Pentecost was a result of unified prayer. The church is at full strength when we have a mind to work together. If ever you find a group working in harmony, one centered on biblical truth, then join that orchestra!

> "The safest place for you is in a place of unity."

THE POWER TO IGNORE

"So I sent messengers to them, saying, 'I am doing a great work and am unable to come down. Why should the work stop while I leave it and come down to you?'" (Nehemiah 6:3 KJV).

I want to introduce to you a prayer that will help you go far in this life. Wanna hear it?

"Dear Lord, give me this one superpower, THE POWER TO IGNORE. I don't know exactly where that fits into the sacred scriptures. Maybe, in the verse that says, 'Don't waste what is holy on people who are unholy. Don't throw your pearls to pigs! They will trample the pearls, then turn and attack you.' (Matthew 7:6 NLT). Or perhaps it's theologically correct to just, 'turn the other cheek.' Either way, Lord, let me overlook the bitter person, the criticizer, and all those who seek to offend. Let me pay no mind to the angry driver, the jealous survivor, and all that feed off drama in general. Thank you for the power to ignore. Lord, it comes to me now, there is a word for it; forbearance. Thank you for reminding me, Lord, Amen."

Forbearance can be defined as having restraint when revenge is easier. Nehemiah and the wall builders have the sense that danger is awaiting them. With great wisdom, he ignored the invitation to meet with his agitators. Nehemiah, with tools in one hand, gestures below, 'I can't come down right now, sorry.' That's about the extent of the conversation. Nehemiah ignores their tricks to allure him. Tobias and Sanballat, along with Geshem the Arab, had a plot to kill Nehemiah.

The timing of their planned assassination is telling. It's a recognizable pattern throughout the Bible. The enemy is aware that he doesn't have long. The scripture informs us that the walls are finished and the gates are almost operational. In desperation, the three cohorts make one last effort to halt Nehemiah's grand opening. What can we learn from this? The closer you get to the completion of your God-given mission, expect an attack. You can be sure that deceptions and falsehoods will try to infiltrate and discredit the work being done. I have learned that oftentimes, your greatest breakthroughs come immediately after some of your greatest breakdowns. Ignore the enemy, don't bargain with him. Just keep focused on doing the good work. Don't come down; there is great work yet to be done. Fight the right battles. Learn to disengage and ignore the ones that steal us from the great work. The Lord's work.

> *"Your greatest breakthroughs come immediately after some of your greatest breakdowns."*

Wanted: a Life with a Purpose

"Those who built on the wall, and those who carried burdens, loaded themselves so that with one hand they worked at construction, and with the other held a weapon." (Nehemiah 4:17 NKJV).

Victor Frankl was a psychiatrist during the horrors of the Holocaust. He was sent to Auschwitz in 1944. Facing humiliation and torture, he found purpose in life by helping others. In his experience there, he noticed a difference among those who survived the experience and those who did not: a sense of purpose. He writes, "What was really needed was a fundamental change in our attitude toward life. We had to learn ourselves and, furthermore, we had to teach the despairing men that it did not really matter what we expected from life, but rather what life expected from us. We needed to stop asking about the meaning of life, and instead think of ourselves as those who were being questioned by life—daily and hourly." (From Internet title: the community well. How did Victor Frankl survive?)

Nehemiah was not facing a mass genocide at the time. But it was a dangerous time when the Israelites needed one another. The walls of Jerusalem meant security for one another. The gate was an emblem of identity. Walls and gates in the Bible are symbols of protection and authority. Walls signify strength and gates typified control. If the nation wanted national sovereignty, they had to fight for one another. They needed the gates and walls completed.

With the enemy planning nonstop destruction for the builders, Nehemiah devised a plan. The laborers and skilled builders were to keep a weapon in one hand and a tool in the other. Could you imagine the fear of being ambushed at any time? The workers and their families faced the mental anguish of not knowing if the enemy was lying in wait each day. Fear is paralyzing. The emotional stress of fear can become so debilitating that you feel like quitting. To counter those fears, Nehemiah assigned watches with weapons. They not only let the enemy know they were willing to protect themselves, but they also became more confident in themselves.

Now everyone of us needs a trowel. That is the symbol of building strong foundations. Building for one another. That is what Victor Frankl discovered; life needs purpose. We are not meant to live for just ourselves. The wall and gates being restored was for the nation as well as the individual. Nehemiah's great purpose in life was to restore the broken places in Jerusalem. Not for fame or fortune, it was for the safety of all. Purpose can be found in helping others. Much like life, our purpose is to protect one another, "to be our brother's keeper." To enjoy life we must at the same time be ready to defend our freedoms. The sword in one hand is what keeps the enemy at bay and their minds in peace. The Bible tells us that the sword of the Spirit is the word of God. It will protect your mind. Quote it! Memorize it! Arm yourselves with scriptures; they will keep you in perfect peace. Just know that when you are looking for the meaning of life it can only be found in Jesus. But, the purpose in your life is to protect and to build for one another.

Victor Frankl said he survived the Holocaust because he sought to help those who were suffering. He was building walls and gates for his countrymen. In return, he survived the horrors of the Holocaust by finding purpose in helping others.

Prayer Focus:

Heavenly Father, I ask in Jesus' name that I may discern the broken-down areas in my world. Let me indiscriminately see the dangerous situations others are in. Forgive me for allowing life's blessings to shield me from the needs around me. I pray that you give me the power to ignore the mental and verbal assaults of the adversary. Give me hands to help others and a mind to work. Father, not on my watch will I let the underprivileged or undeserved be bullied. Make us aware, let us show that You care. Lord, I ask today that you give me another assignment, another chance to do good. With my own eyes let me see the mission accomplished. Amen.

> *"Purpose can be found in helping others."*

Lessons From Daniel

Convictions

"But Daniel purposed in his heart that he would not defile himself with the portion of the king's meat, nor with the wine which he drank." (Daniel 1:8 KJV).

Many years ago, my great aunt, among others, was summoned to testify on an accident. I was young and didn't fare too well. The attorney had me nervous, and I was full of superfluous speech. They intimidated me, bullied me, manipulated my words—I was easy for them. But my aunt, she was another story. My aunt, who endured the Great Depression and many other hard times, didn't budge. She said very little. In frustration, the attorney interviewing her gave up. He said, "If I wanted to keep a secret about anything, I would tell you." She was firm in her convictions; this was a frivolous lawsuit, she believed. She wasn't having it! She was determined. What you believe is the bedrock of your future. You are, in essence, what you believe.

Daniel is a young man, possibly a teenager. His convictions are strong. Peer pressure may be the greatest battle for those teenage years. It could be termed the pressure you have to fit in with the crowd. Daniel showed up in Babylon and was non-compliant. Throughout the book of Daniel, he faced pressure in three areas: dress, food, and music. All were culturally important to Babylon. Do those culturally trendy pressures sound familiar? Today in America, we have the same trends, the same outward expressions of acceptance. In America, our children are masquerading in provocative clothing, the enemy's attempt to steal their innocence. Daniel would not bow to the image as the music played. Today, millions of young people bow to pop music that promotes perversion, immorality. Why? Pop culture is about the crowd, the unseen pull of the world. Daniel settled in his heart to be different. Daniel was a man of conviction. Daniel, through every temptation, said no. As believers, let's stop asking God for successful children and start praying for children with conviction.

22

I Dare You

"He got down on his knees three times a day and prayed and gave thanks before his God, as he had done previously." (Daniel 6:10 ESV).

When we think of Daniel, we instantly imagine lions' dens and panoramic pictures of the future. Daniel makes for a perfect Vacation Bible School set. The growl of lions and fiery furnaces are perfect plots for harrowing dramas. While the former is true, a central theme in the book of Daniel is the battle between the powers of darkness and prayer. Pitted against one another, prayer always thwarts the enemy's plans. The devil despises prayer.

Prayer got Daniel into some dangerous scenarios. If you want trouble, then write out a prayer list. I dare you, go ahead and organize some prayer needs, and resistance will not be far behind. Daniel was unknown at the beginning of the book. By the end, he was a prince of prayer. But be careful when considering Daniel the prince of prayer. Don't just suppose that his feats of faith came with ease. There was a price to be paid. Greatness in any measure must be developed. Be cautious in assuming life was easy for this teenage prodigy. "Great prayer is borne out of great need."

Daniel was from royal seed, high IQ, and handsome. Well-spoken and loaded with potential. Today, we would say there might be the next Nobel Peace Prize winner. We are told from chapter one he is high quality in conduct and intelligence. Daniel is an easy pick to hang out with kings and their friends. But what does any of that have to do with prayer? Not much, really. What did develop him into the trusty prophet? A man who eventually received valuable revelation on the worlds to come. How about instead of the good looks, or being the valedictorian of Jerusalem High, we see him apart from his gifting for a minute. Perhaps there lies the inspiration.

He comes to Babylon with no parents. He has been removed from mom and dad, if they even survived the captivity; he may not know. He saw war up close. His temple has been decimated. Humiliation has brought pain to his heart. The post-traumatic stress of the brutal Babylonian soldiers is a real possibility. Daniel is selected to serve in the king's house as a eunuch, not anyone's first choice. He has lost the ability to have children. His masculinity has been taken. He is learning a new language, a new culture, and he is not even 20 years old yet. He is being threatened to either interpret a dream or die. He is the property of a fickle overlord that is one meltdown from murder. Daniel is a man who has no time for fear. Life has not asked his permission, only that he must accept what he cannot control. Daniel has no temple, no family anymore in which to find solitude.

Picture this! Daniel on foreign sand drops to his knees, looks up into the heavens, and prays, "Oh faithful God of our fathers, help me..". Daniel would pray his way into the history books.

Babylon could not kill him. Lions didn't scare him. Threats and jealous men didn't faze him. How did he cope with the hurt and the tears shed over the loss of family? Daniel found his way home through prayer. Daniel found God to be as present in Babylon as he was in Jerusalem. He found peace in prayer. God is not confined to the temple in Jerusalem. No, he is available even in enemy territory, in captivity, in lions' dens and fiery furnaces. Your help, like Daniel's, is only a prayer away. Daniel dared to pray in spite of the resistance. Just pray, I dare you.!

> *"Great prayer is borne out of great need."*

DO IT ANYWAY

"My God sent his angel and shut the lions' mouths, and they have not harmed me." (Daniel 6:22 ESV).

The signs were posted throughout the city streets: "A Prayer prohibition is in effect for the next thirty days." The latest town hall meeting's topic was the hotly debated prayer prohibition. "Unless it's the king, no exceptions allowed," was the verdict as the meeting adjourned. I don't believe Daniel waited very long before he threw open the windows and positioned his prayers toward Jerusalem. I believe in praying silently, using whispering prayers. I've even used some fast mumbled prayers when necessary; all are suitable and situational. But not for Daniel, not today. He is praying to be heard. So, what does an injunction against prayer mean to Daniel? It means Daniel will do what he always does: pray.

Like a magnet, leadership and jealousy seem to attract one another. Daniel is a leader. He has risen to the top. He is the cream of the crop as far as integrity and character go. Doors have opened for Daniel that others have only dreamed of walking through. His gifting has made room for him at the highest seats. The problem is others want to sit in them. Always remember power attracts many things, both good and bad. On one hand, it attracts people who will flatter you. They believe that who you know is an opportunity for their advancement. That's bad but not the worst. Jealousy is much more sinister. Jealousy is like a weapon in the wrong hands. Daniel's co-regents were supposed to be partners; instead, they turned into vicious enemies. Jealousy made them secret rivals.

There is a penalty if anyone is caught praying to anyone but the king of Babylon. The sentence was a night with the lions, a certain death. Daniel was caught. Overcome by sympathy, the king still kept his word; he kept Babylonian tradition. So off went Daniel into the den of lions.

The same God that Daniel prayed to sent an angel, and the Bible says he shut the mouths of the lions. Here is a powerful lesson: you may be surrounded by those who can harm you, but never forget God is still in control. God may not take you out of the den of lions; instead, He may just insulate you from their attack. What a great miracle. There really is no other explanation. Hungry lions locked in a room with one defenseless man should equal death. No one could deny it. The king was so impressed he had the perpetrators thrown into the lions' den themselves.

I would really like to know what was Daniel's prayer the day he was caught? Maybe it went something like this, "Lord, I know if you have to, you will pull the teeth of the lions out for me. But if not, let them see something more powerful standing in their way." Lions in the Bible often represent us being under a verbal attack, such as gossip, criticism, and threats. Lions roar with their mouths. You may be under an onslaught of verbal assaults. People may ridicule you for your faith. No need to worry, for in due season God will "still the voice of the avenger." God didn't pull the teeth of the lion, but He did send an angel and took away the lion's appetite. Never forget that prayer supersedes the enemy's plots. Daniel stayed relaxed in the lion's den. He did not let fear devour him. Relaxing is a mode of worship that waits on God. Interestingly, Daniel may have slept like a baby while the king couldn't sleep at all.!

> *"Like a magnet, leadership and jealousy seem to attract one another."*

IMAGE IS NOT EVERYTHING

"But even if he does not, we want you to know, Your Majesty, that we will not serve your gods or worship the image of gold you have set up." (Daniel 3:18 NIV).

Worship is a universal call. Worship is the vibrations within our hearts to pursue the eternal. There is true and recognizable worship, what I describe as the "willful reaching towards God." The writer of the book of Romans tells us that God is very near. He is near our speech, close to our cries and petitions. The psalmist pictures worship as the tides of an ocean in relation to the pull of the moon, saying, "deep calleth unto deep." Deep inside all of us is the motivation to worship.

Then there is misdirected worship. This occurs when a person worships something unworthy of worship, creating a false image. They worship what they don't understand. Isaiah the prophet declared, they "worship Gods that cannot hear, talk, or see." They are lifeless idols, created by man many times in conjunction with the dark underworld. For example, they seek fulfillment in money, relationships, and success, all leaving them empty, and so the search continues. Sadly, the unbeliever doesn't even realize he is worshiping something while running from the true God. The heart grows delirious and more confused until the ultimate end surfaces: Man worships man! Deadly and dangerous for him and anyone else around.

Nebuchadnezzar is the king of Babylon. He has a vast empire with many nations, cultures, and tongues under his rule, amassed by strategy and force. Inside the king's heart is the desire to be worshiped, created by his own futility. He knows inside his heart he can't answer all things. After a night of dreaming, he is left puzzled by its meaning, unable to interpret a dream in the night. The fact remains, Nebuchadnezzar is limited. So he creates his own God, made of gold, tall and shiny, the perfect picture of a manufactured God. The king incorporates music into the mix. The people are commanded to bow to the golden image. The new religion is going well until a few Hebrews disregard the orders. Their names are Shadrach, Meshach, and Abednego. The worship is forced and manufactured.

What we can learn from this portion of Daniel is that worship is deeply connected to obedience. The purest form of worship is obedience. Secondly, worship is based on love, not coercion. We worship because He first loved us. We worship because he is worthy of our hearts. Be on guard. Don't make your own idol. When man makes an idol, it tends to be attractive. The self-esteem experiment many people come under ends in failure. The beauty that's enduring is the beauty hidden in the heart.

Idols tend to be attention-getters. The image was golden. Great possessions are wonderful amenities. But, don't fall into the trap of letting nice things define you. Don't put them out front hoping for secret worship. Finally, true worship is typified by the three Hebrews who choose faith under fire. Their obedience brought a divine visitor that insulated them from the fiery flames. God appeared at the exact moment they needed him. The ultimate lesson here is, "if you're going to worship something, make sure it has the power to save and deliver you.""

"Worship is the vibration within our hearts to pursue the eternal."

DO NOT BE AFRAID

"Then he continued, 'Do not be afraid, Daniel. Since the first day that you set your mind to gain understanding and to humble yourself before your God, your words were heard, and I have come in response to them.'" (Daniel 10:12 NIV).

In Stephen Crane's classic American novel, "The Red Badge of Courage," the main character vividly portrays fear in the life of a Civil War soldier. The protagonist shares his inner cowardice, running to the rear of the regiment in the heat of battle, serving his time in the Union army with regret. Hoping that a non-life-threatening wound would strengthen his weak conscience. The Bible is full of battles and characters who are challenged to demonstrate faith over their fears. Fear is a natural response when the stakes are high. It's in the midst of a battle that our trust is tested. In times of conflict, perhaps then we are being "weighed in the balance"?

"The flesh is weak and the spirit truly is willing." Jesus made this statement the night he needed his disciples the most, the night of betrayal in the Garden of Gethsemane. The disciples fled in every direction fear took them, off into the dark night, behind the trees, behind closed doors, much like Adam and Eve, fear sent them hiding. Fear always drives you away from your safest place, the place of trusting God. Trust is placing your life in God's sovereign hands. Courage leads you to where God dwells, the secret place of God fixed in faith and courage. God permanently dwells in the canopy of faith. The Hebrew writer clarified it well, "without faith, it is impossible to please God."

Prayer Focus

Father, I thank you for the gift of prayer. It is another gift from you. Prayer is your way of having fellowship with your children. Lord, I know that prayer attracts attacks. Help me stay consistent in prayer like Daniel. Father, I believe that we are created in your image. Let me seek the face of Jesus and turn from every false image that bids for my worship. I worship you today in spirit and truth. In Jesus' name, I pray. Amen.

> *"Fear always drives you away from your safest place, the place of trusting God."*

LESSONS FROM PAUL

DISCOVERING YOUR PURPOSE THROUGH BURNOUT

"And when the south wind blew softly, supposing that they had obtained their purpose.." (Acts 27:13 KJV).

Many years ago, Adrian Rogers told the dramatic story of a ship caught in a violent storm. The ship was being tossed back and forth across the sea, and the fearful crew watched as ocean water flooded the deck. One crewman held firmly onto the ship's railing, making his way to the front where the captain guided the ship. Once he reached the captain holding tightly to the ship's wheel, he looked at the captain's face, and the captain simply smiled and replied, "Everything is going to be alright." The crewman made his way back to the others and said, "The captain said everything is going to be alright." In life's storms, God gives us His perspective in the midst of the storm. Occasionally, we have to tell everyone at the back of the ship, "Everything is going to be alright."

Paul faced tragedy more often than not throughout his missionary career. He was headed to Rome to face the emperor's highest court, but first, he would experience a storm at sea. With an angry ocean beneath them and gale-force winds surrounding the ship, these words appear, "..supposing we had obtained our purpose".. Have you ever had life hit you unexpectedly like a perfect storm? When it's so bad you tell yourself, "My best is behind me?" Have you ever asked these questions because of age or health? Entertaining thoughts and even asking, "Lord, are you done with me? Am I finished here? Is it time to find a different job or location?" These are all questions that arise while traveling the transitory roads of life.

Paul's story is about a literal shipwreck, but from this passage, we can draw some amazing parallels to the seasons of life. There will be seasons where we feel we have obtained our purpose, enjoying a moment of relaxation, knowing that we can sail here for a while, having reached a safe and productive place. Conversely, during a storm, we might receive the message that it's time to move on; we have obtained our purpose here. In either episode, through shipwreck or smooth sailing, we, like Paul, can remain confident that "in spite of the storm, He still has His hand on the wheel."

> *"Everything is going to be alright."*

Your Wounds Are Useful

"But when Paul had gathered a bundle of sticks and laid them on the fire, a viper came out because of the heat, and fastened on his hand." (Acts 28:3 NKJV).

First a shipwreck and next a snakebite. What possibly could go wrong next? That's a day in the life of the Apostle Paul. He survived a shipwreck, only hours later to be bitten by a venomous viper. We often face seasons in our life much like that old saying, "when it rains, it pours." You have experienced it; I have too. Trying times, when trouble is on the heels of trouble. Paul had just survived the storm only to be stranded on an unknown island. Sea-soaked and cold, Paul picks up kindling in hopes of staying warm. As Paul tosses the wood into the campfire, camouflaged on a piece of wood is a deadly viper. The snake bite was witnessed by those huddled around the campfire. In suspense, they waited for the venom to take effect. Miraculously, it never did. Paul calmly shook it off in the fire and continued building the community campfire.

A storm at sea is a prescription for panic. But a snakebite by a poisonous serpent is pure terror. How did Paul hold it together? I believe much had to do with what the Lord revealed to Paul. Paul had been told by the Lord that he would make it to Rome, preach about Jesus and His resurrection to the emperor's palace. So come storm or serpent, he was unshaken. You too can rest assured that what God has assigned to you will happen. His promises are "yea and amen to them that believe."

Lessons From Paul

What we learn from this passage is that miracles follow closely upon hardships. "Disappointments," Dr. A.T. Pierson said, "are God's appointments." Paul, now a castaway on the island of Malta, will experience the miraculous. Here are his steps of faith that I believe are the recipe for miracles. Publius, a chief of the island, had a father who is near dying, and Paul ministers to him, and he is healed. Paul went from a stick "picker-upper" to an evangelist in a few short verses. Here are a few reasons why:

1. Paul stayed busy picking up sticks to keep everyone warm. So, you too can keep working for the Lord in the cold seasons of life. When you build a fire for others, the enemy will attack. Remember, it's not what you're doing wrong that brings about a satanic attack. It is what you're doing right that attracts an attack.

2. When you are on assignment for the Lord, you're not exempt from wounds, bruises, and bites. Just know that the hurts of life have a purpose. A purpose to expand your influence. There is an island of healing and hope beyond every stormy sea.

3. 3. The hand of Paul that was snake-bitten would become the same hand that prayed for the healing of Publius' father. Remember that what the enemy wants to do is eliminate the gift you have by wounding you. Use your wounds for the healing of others.

Difficulties are commonplace for the Christian. Don't shut down; miracles are on the other side of your greatest attacks.

> *"Disappointments," Dr. A.T. Pierson said, "are God's appointments."*

BE STRONG IN THE LORD

"Finally, be strong in the Lord and in his mighty power." (Ephesians 6:10).

In the hit movie Gladiator, we are given a picture of the Roman fighter. The Roman soldier was similar: fierce, unafraid of battles, and highly trained.

The apostle Paul is a political prisoner of Rome. He, at some point, would have been heavily guarded by the praetorian guard. Mike Ricardo writes in his seminary blog (taking advantage of evangelistic opportunities), "The praetorian guard was a company of 9,000 elite soldiers that were particularly tasked to protect the emperor and his interests. Apparently, Paul's case was a high priority for Nero because the incarcerated apostle was being guarded around the clock by the imperial elite. The 'chain' he wore (cf. Acts 28:20; Ephesians 6:20) was an 18-inch long chain that connected a handcuff on Paul's wrist to a handcuff on the wrist of the Roman guard. There wasn't an hour of the day when Paul wasn't 18 inches away from a Roman soldier of the imperial guard." From this close-up view of the Roman soldier, Paul is inspired to write by the help of the Holy Spirit concerning the believer's armor.

Paul cannot put the pen down without preparing the Ephesians for the inevitable spiritual warfare. First, he admonishes them to "be strong in the Lord." What a power-packed statement. We start by surrendering to the King! One of humanity's greatest weaknesses is to put our faith in something or someone else. It's a fallen attribute in many respects, a clear signal of our independence and self-sufficiency. But Paul understood that the Roman soldier derived his authority and commitment to serve Rome from the massive wealth and honor of the emperor, the most powerful man in the world at that time.

Just as the Roman soldier's authority is derived from the emperor, Paul tells the believer to be "strong in the Lord." The believer's strength is a delegated authority. For example, Paul never tells us to be strong in our beliefs, our education, or physical strength. The first step in preparing for battle is to surrender our allegiance to the Lord! The most powerful person throughout all eternity. Our strength is an invisible but active faith in the Lord's ability to win every battle.

In school, we all had our strong subjects. For some, it was math; for others, reading. Paul is saying make Christ your favorite subject! In life, to master or be proficient in any subject or skill, there must be dedication and time spent. Likewise, Paul is stating that we must become consumed with knowing the Lord. Obsessed with the Lord. Be strong in the very subject of Christ! Enroll in the "University of Christ." Take every course on His Lordship. Become a student of Jesus. Make the Lord your lifelong study!

> *"Make Christ your favorite subject!"*

DRESS FOR SUCCESS

"Put on the whole armor of God, that you may be able to stand against the wiles of the devil." (Ephesians 6:11 NKJV).

The first day of school: if you graduated from a public school, you would have had 13 of them, counting kindergarten. Looking back now in retrospect, the anxieties of the first days of high school were not about getting lost between homeroom and first period. The biggest concern was your outfit. The first day was the largest fashion show of the year. Each year, my mom and I would go shopping for at least one week's worth of school clothes. Five days that you looked rich and clean. After that, you mixed and matched. I wanted the football shirt; she insisted on a nice button-up shirt. I wanted basketball shoes; Mom was my first psychologist; she assured me "everyone respects a nicely dressed young man." I came home with penny loafers and chocolate brown corduroy pants. The penny-placing ceremony was fun. What I know now looking back is there was a connection between my confidence and my clothes. That first week I held my books and headed down the hallway like a model on a runway. By week two, reality set in, that learning is what's most important. If you can't relate to school shopping, then perhaps you can see the believer's clothes have some similar analogies.

Paul tells the Ephesian church that they must "put on the whole armor of God." Notice the active verb, "put on," in verse 12 of Ephesians chapter 6. Paul is emphasizing the necessity of being responsible for putting on your armor. The battle gear has been provided by God; it is necessary for you to clothe yourself. Today, the believer must be clothed for battle. During my days in high school, the objective was to impress. Dressing to impress doesn't work in spiritual warfare. The adversaries we face are not concerned with the cost of our clothing. The evil spirits lurking aren't impressed with your appearance. Instead, we must be dressed to defend our hearts and minds on this evil day.

Edmund Burke's famous quote, "The only thing necessary for evil to triumph is for good men to do nothing," warns us not to be complacent. How do we prepare for battle? Through daily Bible reading and consistent prayer. Be in subjection to the house of the Lord. Exercise your heart and mind like a good soldier in the army of the Lord. Being consistent in spiritual training will be beneficial all the days of your life. Finally, this armor will assure that you stand in the fight. Keep standing for something. Stand for truth, stand for life. Stand firm on your convictions. A properly dressed believer will outlast the enemy. As a believer, we must be dressed for success.!

> 66
>
> *"Stand firm on your convictions."*

HARD PLACES

"For the weapons of our warfare are not carnal, but mighty through God to the pulling down of strongholds;" (2 Corinthians 10:4 KJV).

Strongholds! Just the mention of that word instantly provokes images of a medieval castle, at least it does for me. I can picture a dark, musty dungeon with chains hinged to large stone block walls. A dark and damp place, where the sound of water drips into puddles on the floor. Eerily depressing. It is the last place anyone would want to be. That's a physical image, the spiritual portrait is not much better.

The word stronghold, in the original language, can mean a "hard place." A castle in our hearts that has been in the making for some time. The walls that surround us get stronger by the year. A stronghold is developed by not dealing with the hurts and lies that we encounter in the world, being held captive by deceptive and intrusive thoughts.

It was in the midst of competing worldviews that Paul shared the gospel with the world. In his second letter to the Corinthians, Paul is warning those who are questioning his authority. He makes them aware that his weapons originated in heaven, namely prayer and scripture. As well, these weapons can be used to defeat the loud worldviews that are lying to the culture. When it comes to salvation, Paul is aware that warfare takes place in the hearts of people. Notice Paul uses three words that we are to recognize in spiritual warfare. The first is to demolish. To demolish means "to tear it apart and remove it." Don't let anything stand. Strongholds must be removed. You have to pray for the right voices of influence over your children. For anyone to get free, a deep-seated stronghold, their false beliefs must be destroyed by scripture.

Paul next uses "casting down the high things." He could be referencing the intelligentsia of the day, those who hold science above faith. Down the halls of American universities, the serpent hides, dispersing lies of reason and humanism. Paul says these thoughts, imaginations that have influenced our worldview must be cast down. They must be toppled. The casting down, in the original language, is putting the wisdom of the world in subjection to the word of God. Paul is saying, we must deliberately esteem scripture over "high things." Keep the "isms" on the ground; beneath the truth. Victory is ultimately achieved by wielding the sword of the Spirit.

There is no better day than today to recalibrate your mind by the word of God. God said to Jeremiah, "..is not my word like a hammer breaking the rock to pieces?" The scriptures are a hammer forged by the fires of eternity. Use it to break free!

❝

"Victory is ultimately achieved by wielding the sword of the Spirit."

SING ANYWAY

"And at midnight Paul and Silas prayed, and sang praises unto God: and the prisoners heard them." (Acts 16:25 KJV).

I went from a pain in my right side to being told I needed an appendectomy as soon as possible. I was scheduled for surgery that night. At first, I told the surgeon I think I will get a second opinion. I was foolish enough to believe I could diagnose my own pain without X-ray or imaging. The kind surgeon stopped by my room to talk to me. He had heard that I was reluctant to have this operation. He sat down in the chair next to my hospital bed and said, "If this was my own son, I would do this in a heartbeat." I agreed to have the operation. It helped change my mind when he said, "if it ruptures, you could die. Okay," since you put it that way, let's do this.

What I remember most was how much of a struggle I had praying for myself. For some reason, while I was in the operating room waiting, I just couldn't pray. My faith felt stifled. My soul was silent. I wondered why? My answer would come later; I learned that there will be times in your life when you need someone to pray for you. You will need a prayer partner, someone who will stand in for you when you can't pray for yourself. You will need a Silas. That experience brought me a great truth. You will need other people to pray for you. The story of Paul and Silas explicitly says that it was "at midnight they sang."

In the Bible, whenever the word midnight is used, it implies a time of trial and testing. Midnights are quiet as much as they are dark. A season where you can't see exactly where all this is going. It's dark both spiritually and physically. One psalmist wrote it best, "weeping may endure for the night but joy comes in the morning." Paul and Silas had endured a beating and were locked in chains. The easiest response would be to just sit down and rest their wounds. But they didn't. I mean it would be awfully easy to sit and sulk. Or be overwhelmed by just how unfair life is for a couple preachers. Paul and Silas, unlike I did, would sing themselves free. They "shout and tell the glad story." When walking with the Lord He is able to send you a friend for your midnights. Ever have a song flood your mind in troubled times? Have you ever awakened to a song that stayed in your head all day? You see I have found that God sends us songs in our midnights. More or less God sends us songwriters personally to our hearts.

After a while, the Hymns they sang hit heaven and God stood up. The jail shook and the doors swung open. What was it that pleased God so much that He delivered them? What caused this extravagant faith? I believe it was the unity to lift one another up despite the circumstances.

Worship was a comfort to their bruises and a gateway to heaven's miracles. So keep on singing. Sing at midnight. Your prayer may be for someone who can't pray. You may be singing for someone who cannot find a song. Just sing anyway!

> *"He is able to send you a friend for your midnights."*

STAY STIRRED

"Now while Paul waited for them at Athens, his spirit was stirred in him, when he saw the city wholly given to idolatry." (Acts 17:16 KJV).

In 2011, I got the news that my dad had been diagnosed with CLL leukemia. He shared the hard news with us early one morning. He told the family not to worry and to go on as normal. My dad has been a pastor for most of his life. His impact on me is beyond words. The day I received the news, I remember developing a special awareness of evil. It was strange. I felt a deep disgust for sin. I was angry. More awakened to a fallen world than I have ever been. Every secular song, and every unholy thing I heard and seen that day upset me. As believers, we have a natural enmity with sin. Our renewed nature alarms us of sins and its contaminations. But, it is especially troublesome when evil touches the people we love. When bad happens to those that are good. There is a war that is soon to follow.

After escaping an assassination plot, Paul finds himself alone. He was a Jew ministering in Roman-Greek culture. The culture was overly superstitious. Worshiping a plethora of Gods, the culture is a collection of confusion. With 12 main deities and several mini ones, they must have been worship-weary. Before Paul ever stood on Mars Hill to share Jesus, he stood alone. He stood and stared at the coercive deception of idolatry. Paul was stirred.

Have you ever been angry enough to make a change? Paul was stirred in his spirit to use his gift. Where "sin abounds" is usually where God drops us. In essence, "here is what I created you for, use your gift here." I know we want to be assigned a culture of comfort. We love to be exiled unto those with commonality. But the truth is, God many times drops us into a mission field. Sometimes all it takes to make a difference is to be given an eye view of evil that appears to be winning. Masked in statues of stone and wood, these ancient spirits are hiding to detract worshipers from the one true God. Paul is beside himself; somehow the foolishness of lifeless idols can hold such control over the culture. A "stirred" up Paul preaching a powerful Gospel confronts the elite thinkers on Mars Hill. The results reach even to the emperor's place.

What is it that angers you into action? Take note, inspiration comes from being in awe of something. Being stirred gives birth to the awareness that something must be done. There is much to be stirred about today. I have found that the things we hate are sent to motivate. Stay stirred.

> *"Have you ever been angry enough to make a change?"*

The Valedictorian

"I have fought the good fight, I have finished the race, I have kept the faith." (2 Timothy 4:7 NIV).

Paul, the apostle, was the valedictorian of the early church, penning a total of 12 (13 if Hebrews is his writing) books in the New Testament. A valedictorian is remembered most often by their closing speech. When I graduated, I remember the anticipation of turning over the tassel and throwing the cap. It is the traditional way of saying, "I am finished," in the public school ceremony. Paul in Second Timothy 4:7 writes one of the greatest valedictory speeches in all history. The mighty servant of God lets us know he has finished his assignment here on earth.

As often in the writings of Paul, he would end an epistle with a grand finale of wit and wisdom. Inspired by the Holy Spirit, the church has been strengthened throughout history with these victory verses.

In addressing the Philippians, Paul takes the stage while the class eagerly listens. With principals and counselors at his back, he says, "to my class and friends, in serving the Lord I have found out that no matter the challenge, no matter the odds, 'I can do all things through Christ who strengthened me.'"

To all the Timothy's out there, to every underdog, he goes on to say, "..'no man stood with me, all men forsook me but the Lord stood with me.'" (2 Timothy 4). He will help you too! To every student out there I close with this, I have fought a good fight!

Keep fighting, you will win with Christ. "Keep the faith". Hold on to faith if you lose everything faith will keep you. Faith will keep you when you have nothing left to hold onto. "Finish," like every good student, I have finished my course. I have met the requirements that the great teacher, the Lord Jesus, asked of me. Not long thereafter the apostle dies as a martyr for his faith. The scene moved to heaven. Escorted by a roar and a hand-clap, Paul walks across the heavenly platform and receives his diploma. He hears these words, "Well done thou good and faithful servant."

Remember we all can become valedictorians. Your life is a speech that others will be inspired by.

Prayer focus

Father, you have chosen me for your purposes. Thank you for my salvation. You are my refuge and my rescuer. You are the God who fights for me. Today, I arm myself with your mighty weapons of warfare. Keep me in your perfect peace when surrounded by many troubles. "Open the eyes of my understanding that I may know the hope of your calling...". Lord, deliver me from every covert and evil plot against me. In life's stormy seas you are my anchor. In Jesus name I pray. Amen.

❝

"Your life is a speech that others will be inspired by."

JOSHUA

"The question was posed to Abraham Lincoln: 'Is God on our side, Mr. President?' He replied, 'Sir, my concern is not whether God is on our side; my greatest concern is to be on God's side, for God is always right.'" — Abraham Lincoln.

It's not easy to admit when you don't know what to do. The highlights of our life don't normally begin with, "I have no clue what I am going to do?" Or do they? Well, the highlights may not, but in the Bible, the beginning of many great victories started with questions just like that. (It is said that we don't use our brain efficiently and effectively until there is a problem that arises.)

Joshua is a celebrated leader in Israel. He is Moses' successor. Moses is gone. God did Moses' funeral personally. That's pretty important. Moses is deeply missed. With only a few glitches to his record, he is a legend in the hearts of the people. Whoever saw such a victory? Hebrew slaves—without a standing army—followed a plan, a leader, and a meal, with obedience. Just like that, the Hebrew slaves danced out of danger over and over again. They walked out of Egypt with their chins in the air, like someone who just inherited millions.

Moses' big task was to move them forward, to ensure that nobody looked back. Oftentimes, we feel as if the assignment given to us must begin and end exclusively with us. God's plan to move the children of Israel forward meant handing the assignment over to Joshua. Have you ever experienced the will to finish what you started, only to realize that God had paired you with someone else as a successor? How about when God wants you to defer or pass the baton? Can you? That's a battle in itself, realizing, "I can't do this alone." Or maybe I was called to start it, suggest it, or bless it, but someone else must run with it. That's where this story begins. It's Joshua's turn to win. He must learn what all humble leaders do: "I need help!"

Prayer Focus

I praise You, Lord; You have never lost a battle. You bless generationally. I pray for tomorrow's Joshuas, that they may take the land. Let revival come to our cities. Empower every church leader in America to take their cities and neighborhoods back. God, we ask that You give us the inheritance of salvation, in Jesus' name.

> *"He must learn what all humble leaders do. I need help!"*

LESSONS FROM MARY
A SEASON TO BELIEVE

She is Mary, the mother of Jesus. In nearly every city today, somewhere there is a statue in her honor. Many times, an artist would sculpt her with eyes looking down and her head bowed. Mary is the definition of innocence. In western culture, both in our pulpits and liturgies, she is an example of purity. Unfortunately, we only talk about her at Christmas time.

In history, she is forever young; time has not wrinkled her appearance. She introduces the world to baby Jesus. Luke tells us Mary's pedigree is quite impressive. She came from a line of kings. You wouldn't know it. In her gospel expose, Mary is hidden by commonality. She is humble. She is brave. Those are kingly attributes. Her great ancestor David killed a giant. Mary's firstborn son would defeat the greatest giant you and I would ever face, death. At the time of the gospel story, Mary is camouflaged by the struggles of the typical first-century Jewish family. You and I might not have chosen her to carry divinity. But, God did.

In Matthew's gospel, Mary is counting down the days until the wedding day. Like any other Jewish maiden, she is excited about this young man. His name is Joseph. Laying in bed at night, she, like any other young girl, pictures dates, and days of love and laughter. Daydreaming about a successful life together. Plans are made; the dads of both Joseph and Mary have already exchanged marriage covenant gifts. Shortly afterward, the angel appears—

the announcement is surreal. The angel departs; with that, Mary paused and stares at her stomach. Her first thoughts, "What am I going to tell Joseph, will he believe me?" Yet, while Mary wonders, God works! God is assuring Mary by an angelic messenger that this is His doing; she is blessed and highly favored by God.

That's a title we would love to have over our heads, right? Highly favored? Ever thought being highly favored means a life of attainment? Mary begs to differ; favor has little to do with prosperity or ease. 'Highly favored' can essentially be translated 'highly responsible' with what God has entrusted you. Favor is never easy. Chosen by God, Mary allows the same hand that selected her to be the same hand to guide her. We must simply trust God while He works out the details. In the end, Mary may have trusted God more than any character in the entire New Testament. She was the first to believe. Let this be the season to believe.

PRAYER FOCUS

Father, I believe that there are selective seasons in history where you pour out your Spirit. There are times of refreshing that come to us. Now, Lord, we know the outpouring of your Spirit is marked by salvation. Let this be the season to believe. Father, open up the hearts of our loved ones; you have the key. We pray for a season of faith to descend over all the land in this season. I ask in Jesus' name. Amen.

> "'Highly favored' can essentially be translated 'highly responsible' with what God has entrusted you."

Breakthrough with the Attributes of God

The Affirmation of God

"Lo, a voice from heaven, saying, 'This is my beloved Son, in whom I am well pleased.'" (Matthew 3:17 KJV).

Respect is one of our prime emotional needs. Both are basic and psychological desires. Our pursuit of academic degrees reaches up for it. Experience, age, and seniority demand it. Teenagers cry over it. Respect. "Respect is something that is earned and never given." In our nature, we crave both respect and affirmation. There will never be a time or age when you won't need one or the other.

These are the reasons why people respect us:

1. Talent: We respect talent. How hard is it to get an autograph from a quarterback you wait hours for? He has an entourage of security. His talent has demanded his respect to be private. He is inaccessible for the most part.

2. Position: We learn quickly in life that certain positions such as a supervisor, coach, etc., will demand your respect. By the way, it is the most faked form of respect. "Leadership has a litany of lovers."

3. The Relationship: You love them because they are related. They are yours. Despite their failures, school deten-

tions, and poor grades. You love them (a form of respect) because they belong to you. Aren't you thankful that God loves us in spite of us! He claims us as His own. The relationship we have in Christ is a familial bond. There is no bond as strong as that of blood. Paul writes appropriately, "And if children, then heirs; heirs of God, and joint-heirs with Christ; if so be that we suffer with him, that we may be also glorified together." (Romans 8:17 KJV). You may not have everyone's respect, but you have God's affirmation!

THE LOVE OF GOD:

"Whoever does not love does not know God, because God is love." (1 John 4:8 ESV).

"To be loved but not known is comforting but superficial. To be known and not loved is our greatest fear. But to be fully known and truly loved is, well, a lot like being loved by God." ~ Timothy Keller.

Love has always existed. However, there was a time when love had no human in which to express itself. Before dinosaurs, before the Himalayas were shoved upward, before the first lions roared and the first bucket of water was tossed over Niagara—there was God's Love.

Theologians teach us that in the language of Jesus' day, a word had to be developed to express God's Love in the Roman world. The word Agape. A word describing a stubborn—I will never leave you—kind of love. Friends will give up on you. Family at times walks away, but "agape" love never will. That is real love, my friends. "Greater love hath no man than this, that a man lay down his life for his friends." (John 15:13 KJV). For only one person could provide such great salvation—Jesus did it.

The ultimate expression of love is to give of oneself. Jesus gave His life because He loved you and me. Karl Barth, the famous theologian, studied every religion and came to this conclusion "Christianity has the God that Loves." "For God so loved the world that he gave his one and only Son, that whoever believes in him shall not perish but have eternal life." (John 3:16 NIV).

IN AWE OF GOD

"Let all the earth fear the LORD; let all the inhabitants of the world stand in awe of Him." (Psalms 33:8 NKJV).

The fear of God is maintained in three ways. Let's define what the fear of God is: It is being in AWE of who God is. Awe is a sense of amazement and adoration, to be overcome by His greatness.

1. Consistent Bible Reading: By consistently reading the Bible, a healthy fear is implanted in our hearts. "That scroll is to remain at his side at all times; he is to study it every day so that he may learn what it means to fear his God.." (Deuteronomy 16:19).

2. Recognizing God's Tests: By recognizing God hands out tests." Moses said to the people, 'Do not be afraid; for God has come in order to test you, and in order that the fear of Him may remain with you, so that you may not sin.'" (Exodus 20:20).

3. Experiential Deliverance or Miracle: An experiential deliverance or miracle. You might say, "Only God could have done that." "It was over for me, but God stepped in." "I was plucked out of danger by the hand of God." In response, we stand in honor or awe of His great power. "Let the whole earth fear the Lord; let all the inhabitants of the world stand in awe of him." (Psalms 33:8 CSB).

THE FATHERHOOD OF GOD

"And Abraham said, My son, God will provide himself a lamb for a burnt offering: so they went both of them together." (Genesis 22:8, KJV).

My first sermon was in an empty church. I would imitate my dad, using a song he and my mom would sing as my material. I preached for about thirty seconds, then ran back to the glass doors, making sure no one was pulling into the parking lot, then repeated the process. I was unknowingly following the faith of my father. In this age of cultural confusion, we need someone to imitate. Sadly, mentors are missing. Instead of fathering a generation of sons and daughters, we opt for a spiritual form of foster care, such as "daddy sports," "poppa academia," and "father iPhone." We find ourselves, once again, at a point in history similar to when Adam lost the face and features of God.

I am of the opinion that Adam strained to hold the image of God in his memory bank for as long as possible. Once he lost the physical visitations of Abba Father, the face of God faded from his mind, only to be recovered by scripture and rescued in the person of Jesus Christ—the image of the Father. Without exception, we need a clearer picture of our Heavenly Father. Not a coach, role model, or even a preacher, but a sharper image of fatherhood. May a father's heart be implanted in us.

In Western culture, fathers are farther away now from the original intention of fatherhood than half a century ago, resulting in the worst of all—a self-made and self-centered man. What are we to do? Let's start by handing out some of Jacob's colorful coats to our children. Take time with our children, personally drape the robe of favor over their shoulders. Like Abraham, let them see us go to the mountain of worship and watch God provide. When Jesus wanted his disciples to know who God was like, he used the analogy of a father. He said, when you pray, "pray, our Father who art in heaven.."

> *"When Jesus wanted his disciples to know who God was like, he used the analogy of a father."*

THE FAITHFULNESS OF GOD

"But Samuel replied, 'What is more pleasing to the LORD: your burnt offerings and sacrifices or your obedience to his voice? Listen! Obedience is better than sacrifice, and submission is better than offering the fat of rams.'" (1 Samuel 15:22 NLT).

In the Bible, the faithfulness of God is easier to understand in the light of obedience.

In the Bible:

- Obedience is picking up five small stones when you have a giant in front of you.
- Holding out a rod over a sea barrier when the Egyptians are hot on your heels.
- Walking every day around fortified walls just waiting for them to fall.
- Leaving a comfortable homeland for a city prepared by God.
- Putting your hands on pillars in the center of a Philistine sports arena.
- Praying after the prayer prohibition was signed by the king of Babylon.
- Noah building an ark nowhere near water.
- In your life:
- Obedience is putting away the stones you feel you have

the right to throw.
- Lifting up your hands when sinking in despair is easier.
- Saying no to life's temptations today when just yesterday you said yes.
- Forgiving someone when revenge is in order.
- Choosing to shake the hand that shunned you.
- Obedience is "giving God something to work with in your life."

Your obedience is directly linked to your belief in the faithfulness of God.

A dear personal friend of mine related this story to me. He was desperate for a new church building. He was a young pastor, and they had no collateral. The local banker said, "I can't help you." The pastor went back not once but several times. Each time the banker replied, "It's not gonna happen." He decided to give up. The young pastor had a mentor who was a praying man of God. He was visiting him and staying at home. Early one morning, the man of God out of nowhere said, "Go down there and get your money." He said, "They told me no many times." He went one more time. When he arrived, the banker said no again, but as he was walking out, the banker called him back and said, "I don't know why I'm doing this, but I'm gonna give you the loan." Be obedient—God is faithful!

> *"Your obedience is directly linked to your belief in the faithfulness of God."*

The Authority of God

"For He taught them as one having authority, and not as the scribes." (Matthew 7:29 NKJV).

"No admittance." "Staff only." "Authorized personnel only." We have all read those signs somewhere, indicating that some places are off-limits to the general public. Only qualified individuals are allowed in those designated areas. Though it may make us feel excluded, these limits are necessary. Only trusted employees should have the keys to the store, the cashier's register, etc., for the safety of all. So, authority is both gifted and earned through trust. Often, we reach our limitations because we haven't gained access by faith to the rooms God has for us. Authority is granted to us as we walk in the integrity of our words. When "we practice what we preach," we gain authority with others. It is in the integrity of our hearts that we receive authority with God. He empowers those He trusts!

Jesus said, "All authority is given to me in heaven and earth" (Matthew 28:18), reminding us that Jesus can go wherever He wants to go. Nowhere are we off-limits to Him. He can reach the lowest valleys of depression and climb up the peaks of your pride, if he must, to rescue you. He has all authority in heaven and earth. Access is only denied by our unwilling hearts.

When I read that Jesus taught with authority, was it the way His voice commanded the room? A voice that must have been as powerful as rushing waters. True, but there is something deeper implied; His words had conviction in them. Jesus spoke under the guidance of the Holy Spirit. Jesus had authority because he never wavered on truth. He never changed the message. We must have conviction and stay grounded in the truth. Authority comes by mastering a subject. As followers of Jesus, we gain authority by allowing Him to master us.

It's time we stop wavering on absolute truth and speak what we believe. Start believing you can walk into every room with authority. In the book of Revelation, John describes for us how Jesus holds the keys to death, hell, and the grave. Jesus triumphed in all three locations; we can too.

Prayer Focus

Heavenly Father, Your name is great in all the earth. Your love is unconditional. Strengthen me as I trust Your unfailing love. I put no trust in my performance or works. Lord, Your promises lead me towards Your faithfulness. Should the heavens fail, Your name will hold us up. Lord, I pray for the courage to obey Your voice. There is no risk in trusting You. As I step out into the world today, I know that You are a heavenly Father who cares and understands. It is in Your authority I stand. Let my convictions be strong, and my voice be heard. Lord, help me not waver on truth. I pray against the spirit of intimidation. I will not make decisions based on money, power, or position. I have a Father who reveals His character with me. In the name of Jesus, I pray, Amen.

❝

"God. He empowers those He trusts!"

Passion Week

A.M.: God's Passover, Beginning at Sundown

It has been said, "a lot can change in three days." Preachers' material for sure, a crescendo of crescendos. An amen-getter from the crowd if ever there was one, but Jesus wasn't after an amen; he was after your heart. He wasn't dying or bleeding for a preacher to fill in a sermon; no, he was dealing with eternal matters long overdue. Known as a victorious cliché depicting Jesus in the tomb while patiently taunting death, it is inspirational. In three days, salvation was secured and wrestled fair and square from a spiritual despot. Yet, in only six hours on Passover, 2,000 years and counting, the world was changed forever.

Actually, a lot can happen in just six hours. In six hours, a thief can end up pardoned and be awarded a brand new home in minutes. In just six hours, a young boy can help a grieving mother deal with the loss of a son. In just six hours, a soldier near retirement can make the biggest mistake of his life, yet it's not held against him. In six hours, the very creator who mounded up dirt and made it talk and walk stopped breathing on a tree. A lot can happen in just six hours. In six hours, he can turn the sun dark, and it refuses to shine. Remember, Passover begins at sundown.

Let us redeem the time, even if it's just six hours.

P.M.: THERE IS STILL ROOM

"There is plenty of room for you in my Father's home. If that weren't so, would I have told you that I am on my way to get a room ready." (John 14:2 MSG).

Ira Stanphill wrote over 500 gospel songs. He conducted revivals across 40 countries. The story goes that often he would hand out slips of paper at his services and ask for the congregation to submit suggestions for a new song title. One request impressed him; the title suggestion was "There is room at the cross for you." Soon after, Ira Stanphill penned the words to that song. Years later, while the song was making its way outside an open crusade, a young man lost in depression and on his way to commit suicide was moved by the words of that song. The man was drawn inside the meeting and away from the thought of suicide. He would give his life to Christ and eventually became an evangelist himself. Excerpts from Diana Leagh Matthews' "Behind the song: Room at the Cross for You."

The story sheds much admiration upon Ira Stanphill, and rightfully so. I mean, 500 songs written and recorded is quite a feat. I struggle to write my first. The booming voice of the worship leader that carried through the night and into a hurting heart is impressive. If only I could relate, but I can't; my singing doesn't boom, it more or less squeals in and out of key.

But for me, it's the anonymous man or woman who handed in the slip I want to know more about. The one character in the above story that I want to meet is the one who took the pencil or pen and scribbled on a piece of notebook paper the song idea in the first place. A meet and greet of the very author who introduced the thought, "there is room at the cross for you." I want to know more about him or her. Would they tell me there was a church, a social group, or a snobby clique that said no vacancy here? Keep moving! Was there a definitive moment when they didn't fit in? They could not find anyone who could make room for their mistakes or room for their struggles.

I think the song title was an honest plea. A testimony. Maybe, no one had room for the person who drafted that song, but Jesus. Jesus understood a "no room at the inn" feeling. Have you ever felt like there is no room for you anywhere? You don't fit in? Hear the words of Jesus while teaching over a table of bread and wine. I picture his arms extended wide while his disciples listen, "there is room for everyone at my Father's house" John 14:2 MSG. It is one of the first universal altar calls in the gospels, "there is still plenty of room." Room for misfits, room for sinners, and so-called saints. There is room for betrayers, backstabbers, and cussing fishermen, doubting Thomas's, and most importantly, there is room for me and you. I think that's what Jesus was trying to say to them that night before the cross. There is so much room at my Father's house, and if I have to, I will prepare a room just for you!

Jesus Went First

"Don't let this rattle you. You trust God, don't you? Trust me." (John 14:1 MSG).

I admit that when it comes to risk or the possibility of danger, I normally don't go first. When I was growing up, there were times I would find an excuse as to why my bicycle wasn't working right. Pedaling as hard as I could, and at about the precise time my front tire would hit the ramp, I would jump on the brakes. I am pretty sure my friends caught on—I always had a good excuse for why my bike wasn't ready to launch the ramp. Bad brakes? A loose sprocket chain? I used them all. The real reason; I was a little afraid. (Not to mention it was built by three or four 10-year-olds). But, I was always happy to watch the neighborhood kids go first.

When we read John 14:1, we sometimes miss the chronology of the moment. It is the center of passion week. Jesus is nearing death by crucifixion. The Lord's intentions are clear. He will go first! As the disciples huddle around the Passover table, Jesus says, "I will go first. I'll face death for you. So you won't have to let death bully you around." "Don't let this rattle you." (John 14:1 MSG).

Jesus is letting his disciples—now turned friends—know, "I am going to go first. I am going to investigate death for you. I'll figure it out. I am going to be the first to take the fear out of dying." Jesus will, by the weekend, remove the shadows of death and replace it with a bright light of hope. In a matter of a few hours, Jesus would not hit the brakes; He would find no excuses. Instead, He would hit death's dangerous ramp head-on. The Gospel story is clear—good men ran, while cowards watched from a distance. For me, nothing has changed. As I read the last week of the life of Jesus on earth, I find myself being the one watching, the one making an excuse. I admire such courage, don't you? Jesus went to visit death first and foremost for all of us.

"Don't be rattled by the fear of death. Just remember, Jesus went first and stuck the landing!"

> *"I will go first. I'll face death for you. So you won't have to let death bully you around." "Don't let this rattle you."*

43

ALL IS NOT LOST

"For this son of mine was dead and is alive again; he was lost and is found." (Luke 15:24 NIV).

Breakdowns come in many forms in life. The last week of Jesus will remedy the ultimate breakdown—the fall of humanity.

Perhaps, we remember our parents saying to us as kids after a bad experience, "It will be okay; it's not the end of the world." My grandson Levi, who is five years old, was bringing some Christmas cookies to me the other night. It was dark out, and he tripped and dropped them on the ground. That broke his heart. While for the moment, it seemed that all was lost, to him, a five-year-old, he was forgetting that more cookies can be made. His mom still has the ingredients and the oven to make more.

Being reminded that in Genesis 2:7, God took ingredients of dirt and breathed into it, and man was formed. Adam became a living soul. But like my grandson's cookies that fell, Adam would fall in the garden of Eden. But God would, in time, gift us a new Adam—the Lord Jesus Christ. In a few days, while on the cross, Jesus would take what was fallen and make it brand new. Because of Calvary, we can now say, "All is not lost."

Written by my dad while undergoing chemotherapy.

PRAYER FOCUS

Father, I thank you for the blessings and benefits of Calvary's cross. I believe you are my healer. Lord, forgive me for running away from your grace. You have given me another chance. You are my redeemer. Your death and resurrection have destroyed the fear of death. Savior, when I am afraid, then I will trust you. Father, I push aside whatever is crowding out my time with you. I make room for your presence to flow like a river in my life. I choose to redeem the time by helping others. Forgive me if I have crowded you out. I ask for more room in your house. Today, may you soften the hearts of my loved ones. In the name of Jesus, we pray, Amen.

> *"All is not lost."*

Roman Soldiers

"After they had mocked him, they took off the robe and put his own clothes on him. Then they led him away to crucify him." (Matthew 27:31 NIV).

He was hiding the moment Adam took his first step. The green grass was lush where Adam walked. There were no enemies in sight, at least for now. Have you ever wondered what a world would look like without any enemies? No threats. No wars. Not even an argument.

A world with no nemesis. A world where only love exists. Wouldn't that be wonderful? Sadly, there has never been a time in the past 6,000 years of human history where an enemy did not exist. The serpent was in the garden. Abel suffered from Cain's jealous rage. Jerusalem was destroyed by Babylon. Rome, the Germanic tribes. Human history is littered with enemies both national and personal. For that, we have soldiers and armed forces whose existence is needed because there is an enemy.

The Roman soldier was battle-hardened. He was trained to do two things: obey and protect. The soldier's oath was to remove any threats to the nation and emperor. The Roman soldiers took Jesus at Pilate's command. They never asked questions, "Is Pilate right or wrong?" They were not asked to agree, just react. What do we see in those soldiers? Sadly, we see you and me. All of us have played the soldier of misfortune. We have overreacted when we should have waited for the answers. Believed instead we doubted. Brought out the whips of revenge instead of offerings of peace.

We do what soldiers do—obey.

Likewise, our flesh can be a cruel commander. The soldiers at the cross were trained to be insensitive. That's who they were. After so much bloodshed, a soldier becomes desensitized. There in their grasp was Jesus, no threat to them. He died for the very soldiers that held him. Each day we must make the choice to surrender our hearts to Christ. C.S. Lewis profoundly said, "Fallen man is not simply an imperfect creature who needs improvement: he is a rebel who must lay down his arms."

> *"Fallen man is not simply an imperfect creature who needs improvement: he is a rebel who must lay down his arms."*

45

SIMON OF CYRENE

"As they were going out, they met a man from Cyrene, named Simon, and they forced him to carry the cross." (Matthew 27:31, NIV).

Jim Caviezel became a household name in the winter of 2004 as he played the role of Jesus in the movie "The Passion Of the Christ." At his own admission, the starring role changed his life forever. Jim became an outspoken believer in Christ. Yearly, at Easter time in America, the classic movie "The Ten Commandments" plays somewhere. Charlton Heston starred as Moses in the classic movie, giving its viewers a Bible lesson on the power of the Passover. He, like Jim Caviezel, said playing Moses was life-changing. What were the transformative powers of such movies? Both movie stars had the weight of the gospel story placed upon them—both came to faith. The gospel is powerful in any form.

There is no way Simon had any idea that his trip to Jerusalem on Passover week would have him carrying a rugged cross. And not just any cross but the most important one in all of human history. Tradition says that Simon of Cyrene was so impacted by the cross of Jesus that he was never the same. He is believed to have taken the message of Jesus back to his native country. What did he experience?

AN UNEXPECTED CROSS

Simon felt the calloused hand of the soldier upon his arm.

With little resistance and in no time, he is shouldering the cross. How many unexpected crosses have been thrust upon you? We protect our Saturdays and family time. Vacations and relaxation are scheduled, but life has unexpected burdens. Without respect for our private time, there is sickness and phone calls and pleas for help. Single mothers and financially short friends all want our backs. Jesus many times lets us feel the weight of others for just a little bit so that we may be awakened to the massive weight he carried that day. Unexpected crosses can be God's way of communicating just how much he did for us.

THE CROSS WAS HEAVY

The cross was a physical weight nonetheless. Sin is heavy. For a few moments, Simon feels the weight of the cross; the questions of who and why such a punishment must have run through his mind. Perhaps, and if only after he was removed from the cross, and walking back to Jerusalem does it dawn on him. Jesus finished the work, and Simon was free to walk away. Salvation was gained by such a heavy price. What Jesus did on the cross gives us the freedom to walk away transformed.

THE CROSS WAS LIFE CHANGING

The cross left Simon with questions. This Jesus of Nazareth carrying a cross didn't fit the picture. Something doesn't add up. Left with questions, Simon searches for answers. "He was innocent, I was allowed to lay down His cross, I went away free, He stayed." The gospel transformation begins when we seek to answer those questions.

> *"The Cross was life changing."*

The Centurion

"When the centurion and those with him who were guarding Jesus saw the earthquake and all that had happened, they were terrified and exclaimed, 'Surely he was the Son of God!'" (Matthew 27:54, NIV).

Something changed his mind. What part of the crucifixion softened the heart of a Roman centurion? He was a veteran of the elite Roman military, displaying uncommon courage on the battlefield and working his way up the leadership ladder. His bravery awarded him the responsibility of having authority over 80-100 soldiers. His job? Ensure protocol was followed. He saw something and confessed that Jesus was "..the Son of God." What did he see? What impressed him? Was it his leadership while under distress?

Leadership

Verbal insults hurled like rocks toward Jesus during the early hours upon the cross. At the brow of Calvary's Cross were several onetime followers of Jesus. "Sure, when the fish and loaves were in full supply, You were our Messiah then." "When the promise of deliverance from our enemies was part of your sermons, we voted unanimously for you, Jesus. But on a cross?" The centurion watches as the crowd leaves disappointed. No argument from the man on the cross. Jesus doesn't say much. He doesn't fire His disciples or lash out at anyone; instead, He forgives. The soldier would have cursed his last words unto death. Jesus holds His composure in battle.

There were miracles. Could that have been what convicted the centurion?

MIRACLES

The ground rumbled; rocks cried out. The sun refused to shine. Something unordinary happened in nature that day. As the centurion stood in the dark, he heard the Jewish king pray from the cross. He died not only for what he believed but who he believed in. The soldier related to such an oath.

Was it a thief's confession?

THIEF'S CONFESSION

There were two of them. It wasn't hard for a centurion to tell the difference; he had overseen a few crucifixions. But he hadn't seen someone offer forgiveness and a new home to someone he just met. Who thinks of other people when you are dying yourself, let alone offer a home with you forever in the next world? Jesus does! A stunned centurion watched Jesus keep his composure despite the crowd's scoffing. He witnessed firsthand a strange day of miracles, probably a first. But, to be compassionate and give such an offer to a criminal? Never in a million years. Perhaps, this was the conversation he heard amidst the earthquake that changed his mind. "Today you will be with me in paradise."

Convicted by the events of that day, his battle-weary heart surrenders to a King on an executioner's cross.

THE TEMPTATION OF JESUS
STONES INTO BREAD

"The tempter came to him and said, 'If you are the Son of God, tell these stones to become bread.'" (Matthew 4:3 NIV).

When an opponent finds the other team's weak spot, he attacks it. Hearts have been taken captive by a weak stomach. Esau lost his birthright due to a weak stomach. Isaac's son lost his right to a ruler's inheritance over a warm bowl of soup. Just about every one of us has had a weak moment—a weak day, a bad stretch where we just aren't as spiritually strong as we could be.

Your opponent knows that. Satan doesn't like your Bible reading, nor hand clapping in church. Believe it or not, he hangs around long after the revival service, waiting for you to get overly excited about money, bored with church, and distracted by social media. He looks for you when you're at your weakest.

Jesus is at the end of forty days of fasting. His stomach has stopped groaning long ago; it's hard to say the feeling of hunger he must have felt. It's challenging to describe what forty days without food felt like when so few have attempted it. We know that food is the source of physical strength. After forty days without food, extreme weakness would have ensued.

Hungry—that's when we are attacked most definitely. Not physically hungry, but emotionally hungry. Hungry for attention. Hungry for success. Hungry for relationships and recognition.

It's when we are weak and hungry that we must be careful of the temptation to fill our own appetites.

I would have loved to have heard Jesus' wilderness prayers. 40 days of prayers in extreme temperatures and loneliness. To have been able to record the words of Jesus in his days of weakness. What did he hold onto? In place of a meal was a verse. A scripture is what Jesus hung onto. And when Satan appeared with his trickery, Jesus used what he had lived on for the past forty days—a sandwich of scriptures.

The wilderness temptation was for you and me. There will be seasons of temptations and loneliness, and we will get hungry. It is the scheme of the evil tempter to open his toolbox of tricks when he finds you weak. In return for the challenge, open your treasure chest of promises. You can hang your hat and rest your heart on what He has written!

> *"The wilderness temptation was for you and me."*

You Don't Look Like a Child of God

"If you are the Son of God," he said, "throw yourself down." (Matthew 4:6, NIV).

With youthfulness comes feelings of invincibility. As we grow older, we know that's not true. At middle age, we attempt to run backward in time, longing to be young again. Unfortunately, the modern fashions we try on don't fit right, even look comical. We've reached a point where comfort takes precedence over style. We look like our parents when we promised never to. Through every age, you've had an image of yourself you wished to maintain. Image is not about how others see you as much as how you hope they see you. This is a false narrative.

Picture this: you daydream about wearing your sunglasses while speeding around town in a convertible sports car with the top down. Not only is it enjoyable to imagine, but you also relish the vanity of being viewed as a success. I can relate.

My youngest daughter's prom night required a nice car. We didn't have anything flashy or sporty. We owned a Prius. But my wife's nephew had the new Tesla sports edition car (when they were rare to see). He offered; we accepted. It was a drop-off for prom pictures and waiting. Guess who got to drop them off? You guessed it! For an hour, I sat in the car waiting. Finally, I got out and leaned on the front fender towards heavy pedestrian traffic, and boy was it busy. I quickly heard two people say, "I like your car." I hesitated, but in my mind, I was in a dilemma: "Should I say it's not mine or thanks with a proud smile?" The proud thanks prevailed. The smile left, and I realized maybe Adam and Eve were just normal. I too was conflicted, awakened by the fact that my image was important, if not inflated.

In the wilderness temptation, Jesus is weak and hungry. Then at that moment, Satan popped the question. He asked it not once but twice. He asked the same old question he has been asking humanity for six millennia. The one that starts with an "If." Jesus left the Jordan baptismal site with words of affirmation still ringing in His ears, "This is my beloved son in whom I am well pleased." Would the same words of confidence be as strong in the spirit of Jesus some forty days later? Adam and Eve in the garden probably questioned it within days if not hours. I mean, after no food for weeks, questionable sleep, the entire wilderness experience must feel overwhelming. Would anyone feel like a son of God while homeless, enduring cold nights and hot humid afternoons? Not to mention the swollen feet as He travels across such treacherous topography.

The attack is sharply precipitated by an "if." If you are a son of God, then why the wilderness? Here is a profile of the enemy you won't want to forget. The devil looks at your external situation, reads your emotional responses to the crisis, and then he attacks.

My moment came in the form of admiration. A midnight blue Tesla and a couple of admirers. I compromised some character for applause. What's your "if"? If they only respected me? If they gave me a chance I could do it better? Are you struggling for acceptance? Are you searching for applause? Are you the quintessential people pleaser? Perhaps, you always have to have it your way? All are signs of weakness! When we are weak, we are an easy target.

The answer can be found by looking in the mirror. Not the one on your bathroom wall, yes, of course, in that one you will see an image that is too wrinkly, and a head with not enough hair. This mirror I am talking about is the one that broadcasts an image of how God sees you. The Bible is designed to give us the portrait, the image of man as God sees him. Between those pages, you will see you as He sees you, forgiven! He sees you as His child. Maybe, you just need to spend more time in front of the right mirror.

"Do not merely listen to the word, and so deceive yourselves. Do what it says. Anyone who listens to the word but does not do what it says is like someone who looks at his face in a mirror and, after looking at himself, goes away and immediately forgets what he looks like." (James 1:22-24, NIV).

The Danger of the High Places

"Again, the devil took him to a very high mountain and showed him all the kingdoms of the world and their splendor. 'All this I will give you,' he said, 'if you will bow down and worship me.'" (Matthew 4:8-9, NIV).

Of all the places that present the most danger to the spiritual person, it is undoubtedly the high places. The "P" word has ruined more preachers of the gospel than anything else, marred more marriages than money, and assassinated more dreams than you could ever imagine; it's the spirit of pride. That's the "P" word I am alluding to. The high and haughty place is a place we all have visited one time or another. The Bible calls it the Pride of life! Illustrated by the proverbial mountaintop experience. How, you might ask? That compliment you take too seriously—beware. The unfounded belief that we are ever that good at anything, period. If you ever remove yourself from this truth—"that it was because of my sin He died," you will land abruptly on the hard fact that we are not that good.

The last attempt of Satan to tempt Jesus is atop a high mountain. There, Jesus is presented with another "P" word—Promise. He promises Jesus, "All this I will give you," he said, "if you will bow down and worship me." (Matthew 4:9 NIV).

Beware of promises that are not in God's plan for your life. Those promises become traps. Not everyone is promised first place in this life.

The Temptation Of Jesus

This last temptation is tricky. Not because of the sheer wealth and power involved, nor the reward for such a lottery of leisure. The temptation is absurd. It involves strange worship. What do we do to remain humble? We Worship! Worship is the oven where humility is forged. Bowing in adoration to the Greater One. But, it is the misdirected worship that Satan attempts to entice Jesus with. We would never worship Satan, you say, never directly, but would you choose a lifestyle of ease over a moment of conviction? Or how about a little dishonesty for monetary gain? Next promotion, next award ceremony—enjoy it and celebrate it. But be very cautious because a tempter may just be waiting on the other side of the mountain.

> *"Not everyone is promised first place in this life."*

Our Final Breakthrough

Three truths about Heaven: In heaven, we will study war no more; family reunions will be ongoing, and Heaven will be a graduation service.

Isaiah 2:4 "...they shall learn of war no more".

Today was graduation day for my youngest daughter. We entered an auditorium full of smiles and a table full of degrees. We arrived early, about an hour early, perhaps to soak in the moment. We skillfully selected the side that my daughter would sit on. We sat near the back row to the left on your radio dial. At 7 pm, the ceremony began. Down the center aisle, dressed in colorful cap and gown, walked the school president and famous alumni. Each gown is adorned with academic excellence.

Finally, out of the hall corridors on both the left and right side, the graduates entered. Some entered happy and confident, some with shy and somber faces. The most consistent expression there said to me, "This is what relief looks like after a 4-year final!" The first turn of the head as each entered was towards the crowd. They were looking for their family. As for me, I was just looking for one. I set in my heart to see her face as it appeared out of the hall closure. I missed a lot of days as she was growing up. I said in my heart I will discipline myself. I won't blink until I see her lovely face. I want to see her first. I am going to be selfish at this moment. Maybe somehow just for me, it will make up for a few missed moments. Near the end she appeared. I saw her first. Lovely as ever. I fought back a tear. I thought about all 22 years of her life at once—this is the greatest land of opportunity in the world.

We can do that as parents. We are given a gift. A memoir, a catalog of mental movies. Of mental pictures that live a lifetime. We can draw on them anytime. Both my daughters have graduated, and in my heart, I know I will relive this moment again. You know graduation feels tied to heaven somehow. Heaven. How we enter is still a mystery. What do we wear? How do we walk in? We are not clearly told. But if the earth somehow stole the graduation ceremony from heaven, or if God sent it down, I wouldn't change anything.

To my family, if I get there ahead of you, I will be in the crowd with a crown. I will look for you first. I will watch for you there. You see, I believe heaven has a graduation day too. Only there won't be seats too hard, nor speeches too long. Only smiling faces and tables full of degrees. Jesus will be the president. The degrees are all the same. Signed by Heaven's president, Jesus himself.

So, if heaven is like a graduation day, I will keep my eyes fixed on you. Till our smiles meet. Keep the faith.

> *"In heaven, we will study war no more"*

ABOUT THE AUTHOR

Pastor Joe Woodyard represents the youngest among three generations of pastors, inheriting a deep-seated passion for teaching. Renowned for his book "Standing in the Shadow of Noah," Joe actively pastors in Milan, Ohio, having stood shoulder to shoulder with his lifelong hero, Bishop Carl R. Woodyard—his father—until his death in early 2024. Married blissfully for 27 years, Joe and his wife Angela cherish their greatest achievements: their daughters, Amelia and Abigail.

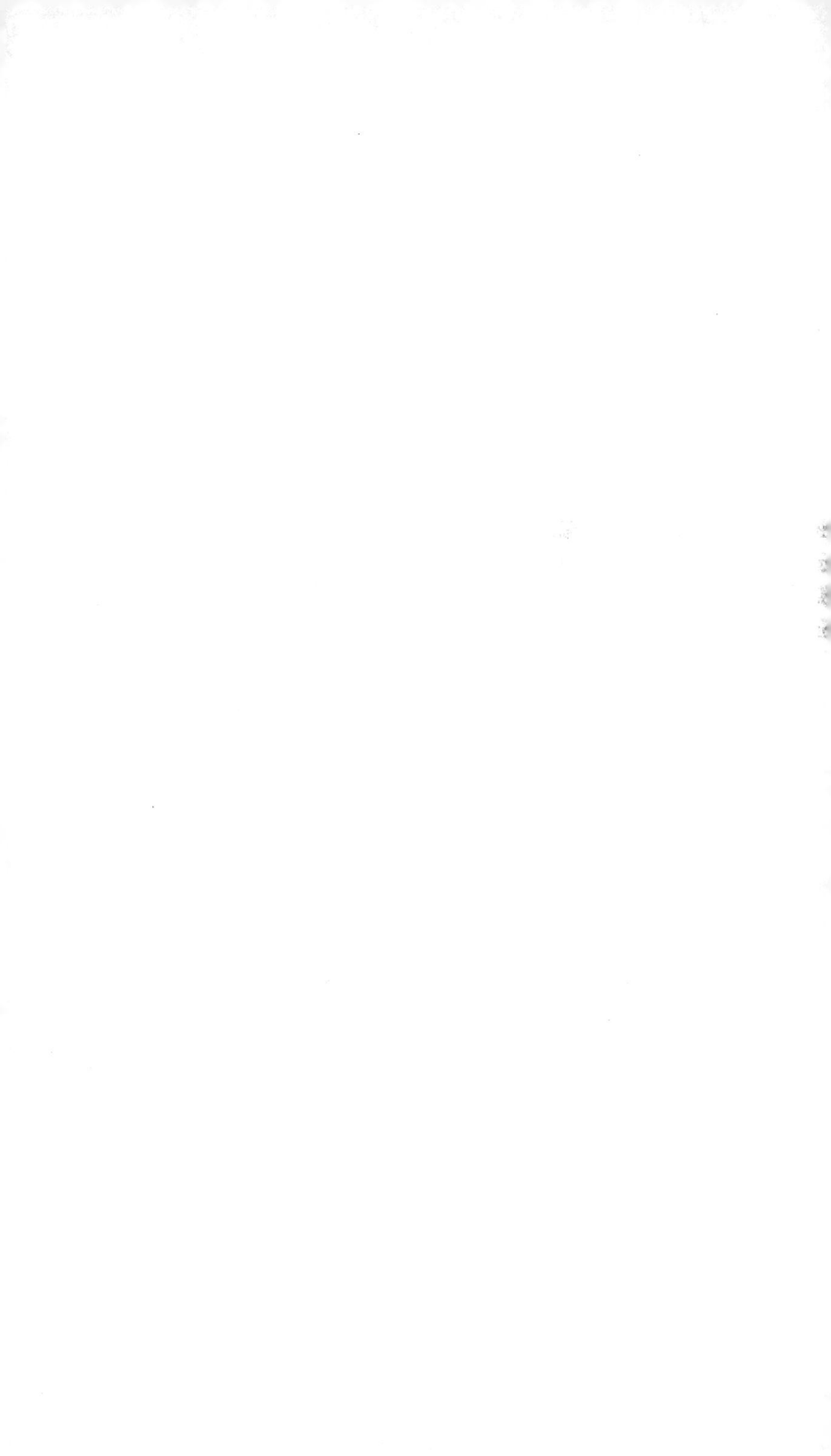